Blood Wedding
and
Yerma

FEDERICO GARCIA LORCA

Blood Wedding
and
Yerma

TRANSLATIONS BY LANGSTON HUGHES
AND W. S. MERWIN

INTRODUCTION BY
MELIA BENSUSSEN

TCG TRANSLATIONS

1994

Blood Wedding and Yerma is published by Theatre Communications Group,
Inc., 355 Lexington Ave., New York, NY 10017.

Theatre Communications Group gratefully acknowledges the support of The
Andrew W. Mellon Foundation, The Rockefeller Foundation, AT&T Foundation and New York State Council on the Arts for the *TCG Translations* series.

García Lorca, Federico, 1898–1936
[Bodas de sangre. English]
Blood wedding; and Yerma / Federico García Lorca ; translated by Langston
Hughes and W. S. Merwin; introduction by Melia Bensussen.
(TCG Translations 5)
ISBN 1-55936-079-8 (cloth)—ISBN 1-55936-080-1 (paper)
1. García Lorca, Federico, 1898–1936—Translations into English.
I. Hughes, Langston, 1902–1967. III. Merwin, W. S. (William Stanley),
1927– . IV. Bensussen, Melia. V. Title. VI. Title : Yerma. VII. Series.
PQ6613.A763A235 1994
862.62—dc20 93-51498
CIP

Cover design and watercolor copyright © 1994 by Barry Moser
Design by The Sarabande Press
Composition by The Typeworks

First Edition, July 1994

Second Printing, September 1997

CONTENTS

Introduction

How strange to be writing an introduction to this book of "new" translations in 1994! These English versions of plays by Federico García Lorca date back as much as half a century, although they have never before been published: W. S. Merwin put the finishing touches on his translation of *Yerma* in 1966, and Langston Hughes translated *Bodas de Sangre* (the Spanish title for *Blood Wedding*) in 1938.

What makes this delay surprising is the fame and reputation of all three poets involved. Federico García Lorca is probably the best-known Spanish playwright in the United States, and the most often produced. The plays included in this volume—*Blood Wedding* and *Yerma*—are part of his trilogy of "Rural Tragedies" (which also includes *The House of Bernarda Alba*). Langston Hughes is surely one of America's most renowned twentieth-century poets, and W. S. Merwin prolifically continues to earn his place in this pantheon.

The principal reason for the publication delay of these exceptional translations is evident in Merwin's history with *Yerma*. When he first approached the Lorca estate in 1966 with the idea of translating the play (at the request of the original Lincoln Center Theater), it granted Merwin permission only for a limited number of performances. No other rights, including publication, were granted.

For many years the Lorca estate carefully controlled the official image of Lorca's writing, and had its own designated translators, mostly scholars rather than playwrights or poets. But Lorca is notoriously difficult to translate. If Lorca's dramatic poetry is not placed in the proper linguistic and theatrical context, his words can come across sounding melodramatic and arch. This difficulty is often attributed to the "passion" inherent in Lorca's writing which, as this argument goes, does not exist in American culture. It has always been assumed that Lorca's plays must overcome not only language barriers, but the greater obstacle of cultural understanding. But why should this be the case when his plays deal with mothers worrying about their children (or their lack of children), and with lovers aching for their forbidden love? While Lorca's plays are set in the context of the regimented society of rural Spain, his themes must be universal since his plays have moved audiences throughout the world for more than fifty years.

It is often assumed that Lorca's characters will never speak English convincingly. This misunderstanding is due, in part, to the view of Lorca as a "folk" poet, an artist as typical of his native Andalucia as the Alhambra and a flamenco guitarist. Lorca himself wrote that his works were not "daring improvisations of my own," but rather "authentic details...it's not often that we approach life in such a simple, straightforward fashion: looking and listening. I have a huge storehouse of childhood recollections in which I can hear people speaking...." And although Lorca's statement is true, it doesn't capture the truth in its entirety. Lorca used the "folk" language that surrounded him as the essence of his work, but captured it through a prism which refracted the words as he set them down on paper. Lorca's "folkloric aspects have been taken as gospel," says Merwin, and his "fancified language taken too literally."

Lorca's springboard may have been the folktales and stories of his childhood, but by his teens he was enthralled by the forces of the avant-garde beginning to flourish in 1920s Spain, and particularly by the Surrealists. Born in Fuente Vaqueros, near Granada, on June 5, 1898, Lorca moved to Madrid in 1919, where he lived in the "Residencia de Estudiantes" and studied at the university. While there he met, among others, Salvador Dali and Luis Buñuel, both of whom became close friends and were to have a great influence on Lorca.

In 1929 he traveled to New York, and later to Cuba, before returning to Spain to write the plays which were to make his reputation. *Blood Wedding* was written in 1932 and first performed in 1933. *Yerma* was written and premiered in 1934. These plays were not only exceedingly successful in Spain, but also in Latin America, where they made Lorca a celebrated figure. However, Lorca's difficulty in reaching English-speaking audiences had begun. *Bodas de Sangre* was produced in New York in 1935 under the title *Bitter Oleander*, and was poorly received (according to the *New York Times:* "What *Bitter Oleander* was like in its original tongue this reporter has no way of knowing... [here] it is overwrought... filled with clipped phrases... nothing comes out of it"). Meanwhile, in Spain his reputation as an artist—and as a homosexual—placed him in danger with the Fascists quickly gaining power. He was assassinated by Franco's army on August 19, 1936, in his beloved Granada.

■

There is no way of ascertaining when Langston Hughes became acquainted with Lorca's work, but their lives followed curiously parallel paths. Although Lorca came from an upper-class background and Hughes did not, their interests and their passions were remarkably similar.

Hughes was born on February 1, 1902, in Joplin, Missouri. His father moved to the outskirts of Mexico City while Hughes was still a child, and Hughes spent much time visiting him there and learning Spanish. Throughout his life Hughes was to continue his visits to Mexico, and to enjoy the company of Latin American artists and writers. In the 1920s Hughes lived in New York City, while Lorca was in residence at Columbia University. Lorca was enthralled by Harlem, and reflected on its people and its music in the poems that were to make up his best-known book, *A Poet in New York*. Hughes and Lorca knew many of the same people in New York, Latin America and Europe, and even idolized the same Spanish bullfighter, Ignacio Sánchez Mejías, about whom both were to write poems. After spending time in Cuba (as had Lorca a few years earlier) Hughes traveled to Spain in 1937, and then to Paris.

In 1938, in Paris, Hughes wrote the first draft of his translation of *Bodas de Sangre*, surrounded by many of the dead poet's friends. There are notes in his own handwriting on the typescript that imply he was thinking of a production—even the name of a Spanish painter he considered using as a set designer. After the first draft, Hughes seems never to have returned to the translation. He was to publish, among his many translations, his versions of Lorca's *Gypsy Ballads*, but *Bodas de Sangre*, which Hughes titled *Fate at the Wedding*, was to remain in manuscript form, apparently untouched until 1984, when I had the good fortune to find it.

I first encountered the translation on a "hunch" of the then-executor of the Hughes estate, George Bass. Bass was a professor at Brown University, and on learning of my interest in Lorca, and in *Blood Wedding*, mentioned that "Langston might have translated that." With Bass's help I was soon able to track down the manuscript at the Beinecke Library at Yale, among the Hughes papers. I then began a process of researching and editing with Bass that was to continue until his untimely death in 1990.

From the beginning my interest was in shaping the text towards production. My final work on the Hughes translation was actually done in rehearsal, in March and April of 1992, while directing the premiere production at the New York Shakespeare Festival. Although Hughes's text was complete when I found it, it was a first draft. There were many errors of verb and subject agreement, many grammatical misunderstandings—easily made mistakes. With Bass's aid I sorted through which were errors and which were artistic choices. Hughes was obviously concerned with staying as close as possible to the original, but also with making changes necessary to capture in English the essence of Lorca's poetry.

I have changed his English title from *Fate at the Wedding* to *Blood Wedding*, since this is how the play has become known in the English-speaking world. However, *Bodas de Sangre* is plural, adding another layer of mystery and tragedy, suggesting that more than one wedding takes place during the course of the play. The original Spanish title forces audiences to look at other relationships in the play, specifically the "marriage" of Leonardo and the Boy in their midnight bloodshed.

These sorts of discrepancies in translation are unavoidable. Aware of this, Hughes took liberties with the original, translating not so much literally as culturally, to his own African-American idioms. Lorca's "Señora" becomes Hughes's "Darling," thereby preserving the warmth, endearment and sense of community implied in Lorca's word, otherwise lost in the literal translation, "Mrs." When Hughes uses the word

"child" for Lorca's "niña," it becomes more than another
way of saying "girl"; with Hughes's language and African-
American sensibilities, the word is endowed with its own
heritage and inflections.

In contrast, W. S. Merwin has written of his desire to
"approach translation as a relatively anonymous activity in
which whatever in the result may appear to be mine comes
there simply because that is how the language, in the always
elaborate given circumstances, sounds most alive to me." So
as to preserve as much as possible the character of the original, he keeps his translations extremely literal.

William S. Merwin first encountered Lorca when he was
seventeen or eighteen years old, and "discovered modern
poetry through him." Merwin, who was born in New York
City in 1927, is fluent in Spanish and an accomplished translator. For Merwin, *Yerma*, like all of Lorca's dramatic works,
"is closer to an opera or a ballet than to Ibsen or Chekhov,"
and his translation reveals this sensitivity, this sense of scale
and musicality. Lorca loved the theatre best when it used music, dance, puppets: the more elements the better, for he felt
that theatre should be a "grand poetic spectacle, the language
given flesh and breath."

■

Although originally the Lorca estate refused to allow the publication of Merwin's translation, in the last few years the estate
has become more flexible, as many of Lorca's better-known
works have entered the public domain. This has led to a reex-
amination of Lorca's work and many new translations, including recent publication of such "obscure" plays as *The Audience*
and *As Five Years Pass*, which had never before been available
in English.

Among all the translations now made available, the works

included in this volume are unique, for they were created by translators who are also accomplished poets and playwrights. In Hughes and in Merwin we have two great interpreters, and although a long time in coming, I hope this volume will contribute to a greater understanding and appreciation of Lorca on the English-speaking stage.

—*Melia Bensussen*

Blood Wedding

TRANSLATED BY
LANGSTON HUGHES

ADAPTED BY
MELIA BENSUSSEN

ACKNOWLEDGMENTS

I am indebted to the company members who were a part of the production process of *Blood Wedding* at the New York Shakespeare Festival, as well as the casts that participated in the readings and workshops, for they helped immeasurably in refining this translation. I also owe a great debt to Kate Rowe of the law firm Lankenau Kovner & Bickford, for her extensive pro-bono work on acquiring the rights to the Hughes translation. My thanks, as well, to the Hughes estate, and to George Bass, who is sorely missed.

Without Vicky Abrash, Bruce Allardice, Constanza Scharff, Arturo Zychlinsky and Charles Epstein, the editing of *Blood Wedding* would never have been completed.

—*Melia Bensussen*

CHARACTERS

Boy	Second Maiden
Mother	Third Maiden
Neighbor	First Youth
Mother-in-Law	Second Youth
Wife	First Woodcutter
Leonardo	Second Woodcutter
Child	Third Woodcutter
Servant	Moon
Father	Death (as a Beggar woman)
Girl	Guests and Neighbors
First Maiden	

Act One

A room in yellow.

BOY: Mama!

MOTHER: What?

BOY: I'm going.

MOTHER: Where?

BOY: To the vineyards.

MOTHER: Wait.

BOY: There's something you want?

MOTHER: Your lunch, son.

BOY: Never mind. I'll eat grapes. Give me my knife.

MOTHER: For what?

BOY: Why, to cut them!

MOTHER: A knife! Always a knife! Knives are no good, like the scoundrels that invented them.

BOY: Let's talk about something else, then.

MOTHER: Guns and pistols and pocketknives, and even spades and garden forks, are no good.

BOY: You're right.

MOTHER: Anything that can split the body of a man apart—
a fine-looking man, with a flower in his mouth, starting out to his vineyards or his olive trees. His, handed
down to him . . .

BOY: But stop talking about it, Mama!

MOTHER: Then that man doesn't come back! Or if he does
come back, it's with a palm on his breast, or a saucer
of rock salt sprinkled on his body to keep it from
swelling. I don't know why you'd dare carry a knife
on you, nor why I leave this serpent here in its den.

BOY: Finished?

MOTHER: If I live to be a hundred, I won't talk about anything else. First your father, like the scent of a carnation to me. . . . Hardly three years with him. Then
your brother! Is it right, I ask you? How can it be that
a little thing like a pistol or a knife can just put an
end to a man strong as a bull? I'll never shut up. The
months go by and still grief stings my eyes and pricks
at the roots of my hair.

BOY: Will you hush, Mama?

MOTHER: No, I am not going to hush! Can anybody bring
your father back to me? Or your brother? The killers
are in prison, yes. But what is prison? They eat, they
smoke, they play guitars. While the grass fills the
bodies of my dead—silent, dust—two men like
geraniums—but the killers sit in prison, cool as you
please, looking at the mountains!

BOY: Do you want me to kill them?

MOTHER: No. I talk and I talk, but it's just because. . . . How can I keep from talking when I see
you go through that door? It's because I don't want
you to carry a knife! It's because . . . because I don't
want you to go to the country!

BOY *(Laughing)*: Oh, Mama!

MOTHER: I wish you were a girl. Then you wouldn't have to go. We could make pretty fringe and little wool poodles.

BOY *(Taking his mother by the arm and laughing)*: Mama, suppose I took you with me to the vineyard?

MOTHER: What could you do with an old woman in a vineyard? Could you hide me under the young vines?

BOY *(Lifting her in his arms)*: Old lady! Old lady! Old, old lady!

MOTHER: Your father would've taken me along. Yes! He was a man, made of good stuff! And your grandfather, he left a baby on every corner! That's what I like. Men to be men, and wheat, wheat!

BOY: Well, what about me, Mother?

MOTHER: You what?

BOY: Do I have to tell you all over again?

MOTHER *(Seriously)*: Ah!

BOY: Don't you think it's all right?

MOTHER: It's not that.

BOY: Then?

MOTHER: I don't know, myself. All of a sudden like that, it catches me by surprise. I know the girl's good, isn't she? Quiet. Hardworking. She kneads her bread and makes her own clothes. But just the same, whenever you mention her name, it's like as if somebody hit me in the head with a stone.

BOY: You're being silly now.

MOTHER: More than silly. But I'm the one who'll be left alone. All I've got left is you. So I'm sorry you're going.

BOY: But you'll come and live with us.

MOTHER: No. I can't leave your father and your brother by

themselves, here alone. I have to go visit them every morning. If I left, like as not one of those Felixes would die, one of that family of killers, and be buried beside them. And I couldn't stand that! No! That I couldn't stand! I'd dig him up with my own fingers and smash him against the wall.

BOY *(Sternly)*: There you go, starting again.

MOTHER: I'm sorry. *(Pause)* How long have you been going with the girl, son?

BOY: Three years. And since then, I've bought the vineyard.

MOTHER: Three years! She had a sweetheart before didn't she?

BOY: I don't know. I don't think so. But girls have to look carefully before they marry.

MOTHER: I never looked at anybody except your father. When they killed him, I looked at the wall in front. One man, one woman—and that's that.

BOY: But we know my sweetheart's a decent girl.

MOTHER: I don't doubt it. Just the same, I'm sorry I don't know what her mother was like.

BOY: Aw, what does it matter?

MOTHER *(Looking at him)*: Son!

BOY: What?

MOTHER: Calm down! It's all right! When do you want me to ask her father?

BOY *(Happily)*: Would Sunday do?

MOTHER *(Seriously)*: I'll take her the earrings of seed pearl, the antiques. And you buy her . . .

BOY: You know what's best.

MOTHER: You buy her some drawn-work stockings. And yourself, two suits. Or three. You're all I've got.

BOY: I'm off now. Tomorrow I'll go see her.

MOTHER: Yes, yes! And see if you can't raise me six grand-

children to make me happy. Or as many as you want
to, since your father didn't have a chance to give
them to me.

BOY: The first one'll be for you, Mama.

MOTHER: Yes! But have girls, too. I want to do embroidery,
and make lace, and be quiet.

BOY: I'm sure you'll like my sweetheart.

MOTHER: Yes, I'll like her. *(She starts to kiss him, then
pauses)* Go on with you! You're too big for kisses.
Save them for your wife *(Turns aside)* —when she is
your wife.

BOY: I'm gone.

MOTHER: Tend that stretch down by the mill you've not
been looking after lately.

BOY: Right!

MOTHER: God bless you!

*The boy goes out. The mother sits down with her back to
the door. A neighbor appears in the doorway in a dark
dress with a kerchief on her head.*

Come in.

NEIGHBOR: How are you?

MOTHER: Same as usual.

NEIGHBOR: I came down to the store, so I thought I'd stop
in and see you. We live so far apart.

MOTHER: It's twenty years now since I've been up to the
end of this street.

NEIGHBOR: But you're all right here.

MOTHER: Do you think so?

NEIGHBOR: So many things happen outside! Two days ago,
they brought my neighbor's son home with both arms
cut off by a machine. *(She sits down)*

MOTHER: Rafael?

NEIGHBOR: Yes. You see! I often think your son and mine are better off where they are, asleep, resting, than to live helpless like he'll be.

MOTHER: Keep quiet! We make up such ideas, but they don't comfort us.

NEIGHBOR *(Sighing)*: Ah.

MOTHER: Ah!

NEIGHBOR *(Pause. Sadly)*: And your son?

MOTHER: Gone out.

NEIGHBOR: He finally bought the vineyard.

MOTHER: He was fortunate.

NEIGHBOR: Now he'll get married, I guess.

MOTHER *(As though suddenly awaking, drawing her chair near the chair of the neighbor-woman)*: Say!

NEIGHBOR *(In confidence)*: What is it?

MOTHER: Do you know my son's sweetheart?

NEIGHBOR: She's a good girl.

MOTHER: Yes, but . . .

NEIGHBOR: But nobody knows her well. She lives way off there alone with her father, ten leagues from the nearest house. But she's good. And used to being by herself.

MOTHER: Who was her mother?

NEIGHBOR: I knew her mother. Beautiful, with a face shining like a saint's. But I never liked her. She didn't care a thing about her husband.

MOTHER *(Surprised)*: Folks seem to know a mighty lot!

NEIGHBOR: Excuse me! It's not that I want to hurt anybody's memory, but it's true. But whether or not she was decent isn't mentioned anymore. Nobody talks about her now. And she was proud!

MOTHER: But you're still talking about her.

NEIGHBOR: You asked me to!

MOTHER: I just wish that no one knew anything about the dead one or the living one. I want them to be like two thistles that nobody mentions, and that prick if they're fooled with.

NEIGHBOR: You're right. Your son is a fine boy.

MOTHER: A fine boy! That's why I look after him. But they tell me that girl has had a sweetheart before.

NEIGHBOR: She must have been about fifteen then, I guess. But he married her cousin ten years ago. That I know. And now nobody remembers their going together.

MOTHER: How do you remember it?

NEIGHBOR: What questions you ask a person!

MOTHER: Well, everybody likes to know about things that touch them. Who was her sweetheart?

NEIGHBOR: Leonardo.

MOTHER: What Leonardo?

NEIGHBOR: Leonardo, one of the Felixes.

MOTHER *(Rising)*: One of the Felixes?

NEIGHBOR: But what did Leonardo have to do with any of it? He was eight years old when those things happened.

MOTHER: You're right. But when I hear the name of Felix, and it's those Felix, *(Under her breath)* the word fills my mouth with mud, *(Spitting)* and I have to spit! I have to spit to keep from killing!

NEIGHBOR: Be calm! What good is all this?

MOTHER: None. But you have to understand!

NEIGHBOR: Don't block your son's happiness. Don't say anything to him. You're old. I'm old, too. It's time now for you and me to keep quiet.

MOTHER: I won't tell him anything.

NEIGHBOR *(Kissing her)*: Not anything.

MOTHER *(Quietly)*: What things do happen . . .

NEIGHBOR: I'm going now. My folks will be back from the fields soon.

MOTHER: What do you think of this heat today?

NEIGHBOR: The children carrying water to the reapers are sunburned as can be! Goodbye, darling. *(She exits)*

MOTHER: Goodbye.

> *The mother goes toward a door at the left. Halfway she stops and slowly crosses herself.*
>   *Curtain.*

SCENE TWO

A rose-colored room, copper plates, bunches of paper flowers. In the center, a table with a tablecloth. It is morning.
   The mother-in-law of Leonardo has a baby in her arms. She rocks it. The wife, in another corner of the room, is knitting.

MOTHER-IN-LAW:
> Little child, little child
> on a big horse
> that won't drink water.
> Under the branches
> the water is black.
> When it gets to the bridge
> it stops to sing.
> Who knows, child,
> what the water says,
> dragging its long train
> down the green halls?

WIFE *(Softly)*:
> Sleep, little pink.
> The horse won't drink.

MOTHER-IN-LAW:
> Sleep, little rose.
> The horse starts to cry.
> His hooves are bruised
> and his mane is frozen
> and between his eyes
> is a silver dagger.
> They went to the river.
> Oh, see them go down
> where the blood flows fast,
> faster than the water.

WIFE:
> Sleep, little pink.
> The horse won't drink.

MOTHER-IN-LAW:
> Sleep, little rose.
> The horse is crying.

WIFE:
> His warm nose
> flecked with silver foam,
> doesn't want to touch
> the damp bank of the river.
> He neighs toward the hard mountains
> with the dead river around his neck.
> Oh, mighty horse that wants no water.

Oh, sharp pain of snow!
Horse born of the dawn!

MOTHER-IN-LAW:

Stay away! Don't come!
We'll close our windows
with branches of dreams
and dreams of long branches.

WIFE:

The child is asleep.

MOTHER-IN-LAW:

My child is still.

WIFE:

Horse, my child has a pillow.

MOTHER-IN-LAW:

And a cradle of steel.

WIFE:

And a coverlet of fine linen.

MOTHER-IN-LAW:

Little child, little child!

WIFE:

Oh, mighty horse that doesn't want to drink!

MOTHER-IN-LAW:

Stay away! Don't come in!
Go off to the mountains,

through the gray valleys
where the ponies are.

WIFE *(Looking)*:
   My child is asleep.

MOTHER-IN-LAW:
   My child is resting.

WIFE *(Softly)*:
   Sleep, little pink.
   The horse won't drink.

MOTHER-IN-LAW *(Very quietly, taking the child up)*:
   Sleep, little rose.
   The horse is crying.

She exits with the child. Leonardo enters.

LEONARDO: Where's the baby?

WIFE: Asleep.

LEONARDO: He wasn't well yesterday, crying all night.

WIFE *(Gaily)*: Today he's like a flower. And how are you?
   Have you been to the blacksmith's?

LEONARDO: I've just come from there. Would you believe
   that for the past two months I've been putting new
   shoes on that horse, and they're always falling off? It
   looks like the stones must pull them off.

WIFE: It isn't because you ride him a lot?

LEONARDO: No, I almost never ride him.

WIFE: Yesterday the neighbors said they saw you way off on
   the edge of the plain.

LEONARDO: Who told you that?

WIFE: The women out gathering herbs. I was surprised to hear it. Was it really you?

LEONARDO: No. What do you think I'd be doing out there in that desert?

WIFE: That's what I wondered. But your horse was dripping with sweat.

LEONARDO: Did you see it?

WIFE: No, but my mother did.

LEONARDO: Is she in there with the baby?

WIFE: Yes. Wouldn't you like some lemonade?

LEONARDO: With some good cold water.

WIFE: Since you didn't come to eat . . .

LEONARDO: I was out with the men measuring the wheat. There's always something to hold a man up.

WIFE *(Making the lemonade. Very tenderly)*: Are they paying a good price?

LEONARDO: Good enough.

WIFE: I need a new dress. And the baby needs a little bonnet with strings.

LEONARDO: I'm going to take a look at him.

WIFE: Be careful, he's asleep.

MOTHER-IN-LAW *(Entering)*: Who's been running that horse like that? He's tied down there with his eyes bucked out like he saw the end of the world!

LEONARDO *(Shortly)*: Me.

MOTHER-IN-LAW: Excuse me! He's your horse.

WIFE *(Timidly)*: He's been out with the men measuring the wheat.

MOTHER-IN-LAW: The horse can drop dead, as far as I'm concerned.

WIFE: Here's the lemonade. Is it cold enough?

LEONARDO: Yes.

WIFE: You know my cousin's about to be asked for in marriage?

LEONARDO: When?

WIFE: Tomorrow. The wedding will be within a month. I hope they'll invite us.

LEONARDO *(Solemnly)*: I don't know.

MOTHER-IN-LAW: I don't think the boy's mother is very much pleased with that marriage.

LEONARDO: Maybe she's right. At least, she's careful.

WIFE: I don't like for you to speak that way about a decent girl.

MOTHER-IN-LAW: Whatever Leonardo says about her, he knows. Wasn't he her sweetheart for three years?

LEONARDO: But I quit her. *(To his wife)* Are you getting ready to cry? Cut it out! *(He pulls her hands down roughly from her face)* Let's go look at the baby.

They exit embracing. A child, with pigtails flying, enters gaily, running.

CHILD: Oh, listen...

MOTHER-IN-LAW: What's happened?

CHILD: The young man came down to the store and bought out the best of everything there was.

MOTHER-IN-LAW: Did he come by himself?

CHILD: No, with his mother. She's tall and serious. *(Imitates her)* But such style!

MOTHER-IN-LAW: They are folks of means.

CHILD: They bought openwork stockings. Oh, what stockings! Every girl's dream of stockings. Look! A swallow here *(Shows her ankle)*, and here a boat *(Shows her leg)*, and here a rose! *(Shows her thigh)*

MOTHER-IN-LAW: Child!

CHILD: A rose with stem and stamen even! Oh! And all in silk!

MOTHER-IN-LAW: Two solid incomes getting together there.

Leonardo and his wife come in.

CHILD *(To them)*: I came to tell you what they're buying.
LEONARDO: We're not interested.
WIFE: Let her go ahead.
MOTHER-IN-LAW: Leonardo doesn't want to hear about it.
CHILD: Oh! *(Going out crying)* I'm sorry.
MOTHER-IN-LAW: What good reason have you got for aggravating everybody?
LEONARDO *(Sitting down)*: Did I ask for your advice?
MOTHER-IN-LAW: All right!

Pause.

WIFE *(To Leonardo)*: What's the matter? What's burning inside your head? Don't keep me wondering like this, without knowing what it is.
LEONARDO: Leave me alone.
WIFE: No. I want you to look at me, and tell me what it is.
LEONARDO: Oh, get away! *(He rises)*
WIFE: Dear, where are you going?
LEONARDO *(Sharply)*: Can't you keep quiet?
MOTHER-IN-LAW *(To her daughter, firmly)*: Hush!

Leonardo exits.

I hear the baby.

The mother-in-law exits and returns with the baby in her arms. The wife remains standing, not moving.

His hooves are bruised. His mane is frozen.
Between his eyes is a silver dagger.
They went down to the river.
Oh, see them go down where the blood flows fast,
faster than the water.

WIFE *(Turning, as in a dream)*:
Sleep, little pink.
Now the horse'll drink.

MOTHER-IN-LAW:
Sleep, little rose.
The horse is crying.

WIFE:
Little child, little child!

MOTHER-IN-LAW:
Mighty horse that won't drink.

WIFE:
Stay away! Don't come in!
Go off to the mountains.
Oh, pain of white snow.
Horse born of the dawn.

MOTHER-IN-LAW *(Crying)*:
My child is asleep.

WIFE *(Crying as she nears the child)*:
My child is resting.

MOTHER-IN-LAW:
> Sleep, little pink.
> The horse won't drink.

WIFE *(Crying as she leans on the table)*:
> Sleep, little rose.
> The horse is crying.

Curtain.

SCENE THREE

Interior of a house dug into a cliff, where the girl lives. At the back, a cross of big red flowers. Arched doorways with lace curtains and red loops. On the hard white walls there are open fans, blue potteries, small mirrors.

The servant, very humble and full of guile, admits the boy and his mother. The mother is dressed in black satin and wears a lace mantilla. The boy wears a black velveteen suit and a big gold chain.

SERVANT: Come in. Won't you sit down? They'll be right out.

> *The servant exits. The boy and his mother sit like two statues, without moving. There is a long pause.*

MOTHER: Did you bring your watch?

BOY: Yes, I did. *(He takes it out and looks at it)*

MOTHER: We've got to be back on time. These folks live so far!

BOY: But there's some good land out this way.

MOTHER: Good, but too isolated. Four hours on the road, and not a house, not a tree.

BOY: These are plains.

MOTHER: But your father would have covered them with trees.

BOY: Without water?

MOTHER: He would have found it. The three years that we were married, he planted ten cherry trees. *(Remembering)* Three walnut trees down by the mill. A whole vineyard. And a plant called the Jupiter plant with red flowers, that dried up. *(Pause)*

BOY *(Thinking of his sweetheart)*: I guess she's dressing.

The father of the girl enters. He is old, with shining white hair. His head is bowed. The mother and the boy rise and shake hands silently.

FATHER: A long time on the road?

MOTHER: Four hours. *(Sitting down)*

FATHER: You must have come the long way.

MOTHER: I'm too old now to come over the cliff above the river.

BOY: She gets dizzy.

FATHER: We had a good crop of alfalfa this year.

BOY: Good is right.

FATHER: In my time this land wouldn't even give alfalfa. You had to prod it and even cry over it to make it produce anything worthwhile.

MOTHER: But not now. Don't complain, though. I didn't come to ask you for anything.

FATHER *(Smiling)*: You're richer than I am. Vineyards are worth money. Each young plant's a silver coin. But what I'm sorry about, you know, is that our lands are separated. I'd like it all to be together. For there's one thorn in my heart, and that's this little green spot here in the midst of my land, that they won't sell me for all the gold in the world.

BOY: There's always one place like that.

FATHER: If only forty pairs of oxen could drag your grape-vines over here and put them on my hillside, how good it would be!

MOTHER: Why?

FATHER: What's mine is hers, and what's yours is his. That's why. To have it all together would be fine!

BOY: And less work.

MOTHER: When I die, then you can sell that over there, and buy on this side.

FATHER: Sell? Sell? Bah! Buy, woman, buy all of it! If I'd had sons, I'd have bought all this whole mountain right down to the river. It's not good land, but with strong arms you can make it good. And since nobody passes along this way, they don't steal your fruit, and you can sleep in peace.

MOTHER: You know why I'm here.

FATHER: Yes.

MOTHER: Well?

FATHER: They've settled it among themselves.

MOTHER: My son is capable, and will do the right thing.

FATHER: My daughter also.

MOTHER: My son is handsome. He's never had a woman. He's as clean as a sheet in the sun.

FATHER: I can say the same for mine. She's up making bread before day, with the morning star. She never talks. Gentle as a lamb. Does all kinds of embroidery, and can bite a cord in two with her teeth.

MOTHER: God bless this house!

FATHER: God bless us!

The servant enters with two trays, wine glasses on one and sweets on the other.

MOTHER *(To her son)*: When do you want the wedding?

BOY: Next Thursday.

FATHER: The very day when she's exactly twenty-two years old.

MOTHER: Twenty-two! My oldest son would be that age if he had lived. And he would have lived, too, strong and manly as he was, if men had never invented pistols.

FATHER: But you mustn't think about that now.

MOTHER: Every minute I think about it. Just put yourself in my shoes.

FATHER: Then we'll have it on Thursday, will we?

BOY: We will.

FATHER: The bride and the groom and ourselves, we'll go in a carriage to the church, because it's a good distance. And the guests in carts, or on whatever horses they bring.

MOTHER: Very well.

FATHER *(To the servant as she passes)*: Tell her she may come in now. *(To the mother)* I will be very pleased if you like her.

The girl enters modestly, her head down, her hands at her sides.

MOTHER: Come here. Are you happy?

GIRL: Yes, ma'am.

FATHER: You mustn't be so solemn about it, then. After all, she'll be your mother.

GIRL: I am happy. When I said *yes*, it was because I wanted to say *yes*.

MOTHER: Naturally. *(Lifting her chin)* Look at me.

FATHER: She looks exactly like my wife did.

MOTHER: Yes? What beautiful eyes! Do you know what marriage is, child?

GIRL *(Solemnly)*: I know.

MOTHER: One man, children, and a wall two feet thick between you and everything else.

BOY: Need there be anything else?

MOTHER: No. Let the others live as they will. Yes, let all live.

GIRL: I'll do my part.

MOTHER: Here are some presents for you.

GIRL: Thank you.

FATHER: Won't you eat something?

MOTHER: I shan't. *(To her son)* How about you?

BOY: I'll take something.

The boy takes a sweet. The girl another.

FATHER *(To the boy)*: Some wine?

MOTHER: He never touches it.

FATHER: All the better.

There is a pause. They all stand.

BOY *(To his sweetheart)*: I'll be back tomorrow.

GIRL: What time?

BOY: Five o'clock.

GIRL: I'll wait for you.

BOY: Soon as I get away from you, nothing interests me. It's like there was a knot in my throat.

GIRL: When you're my husband, it won't be like that.

BOY: That's what I say.

MOTHER: Let us be off. The sun waits for no man. *(To the father)* The agreement is fixed?

FATHER: It is fixed.

MOTHER *(To the servant)*: Goodbye.

SERVANT: God bless you!

The mother kisses the girl and begins to exit with the boy, in silence.

MOTHER *(At the door)*: Goodbye, daughter.

The girl waves her hand.

FATHER: I'll go out with you.

They exit.

SERVANT: I'm dying to see the presents.

GIRL *(Sharply)*: Get away.

SERVANT: Oh, darling! Show them to me.

GIRL: I don't want to.

SERVANT: Anyway, the stockings. They say they are all drawn-work! My!

GIRL: I said, no!

SERVANT: For heaven's sake! All right! It looks like you don't want to get married.

GIRL *(Biting her nails angrily)*: Oh!

SERVANT: Child! Baby, what's the matter? Do you hate to give up living like a queen? Don't dwell on unpleasant things. Have you any reason to? None. Let's look at the presents. *(Takes the box)*

GIRL *(Catching her by the wrists)*: Leave them alone!

SERVANT: Oh!

GIRL: Leave them alone, I said!

SERVANT: You're stronger than a man.

GIRL: Haven't I done a man's work? I wish I was a man!

SERVANT: Don't talk like that!

GIRL: Hush, I said! Let's talk about something else.

The scene darkens gradually. A long pause.

SERVANT: Did you hear a horse last night?

GIRL: What time?

SERVANT: At three o'clock.

GIRL: It must've been some horse running loose from the pack.

SERVANT: No, it had a rider.

GIRL: How do you know?

SERVANT: Because I saw him. He stopped at your window. That's what struck me.

GIRL: Couldn't it have been my sweetheart? Sometimes he comes by as late as that.

SERVANT: No.

GIRL: You saw him?

SERVANT: Yes.

GIRL: Who was it?

SERVANT: Leonardo.

GIRL *(Loudly)*: It's a lie! It's a lie! Why would he come here?

SERVANT: He came.

GIRL: Shut up! Shut that damn mouth of yours!

There is the sound of a horse drawing near. The servant goes to the window.

SERVANT: Come here and look! Was it him?

GIRL: It was him!

Quick curtain.

Act Two

SCENE ONE

Courtyard of the girl's house. At the back, a huge arched doorway. It is night, shortly before dawn.

   The girl appears followed by the servant. Both are in starched white petticoats of lace and embroidery, and white corset covers, with their arms bare.

SERVANT: I'll finish combing your hair here.

GIRL: It's so hot you can't stay inside.

SERVANT: In this part of the country it's not even cool at dawn.

   The girl sits in a low chair and looks at herself in a hand-mirror. The servant combs the girl's hair.

GIRL: My mother was from a section where there were lots of trees. A rich land.

SERVANT: That's what made her so lively.

GIRL: But she got burned out here.

SERVANT: Fate!

GIRL: As we all are burned-out. These very walls shoot
flames. *(Jerking her head)* Oh! Don't pull so!
SERVANT: I'm trying to fix that curl better. I want it to fall
just over your forehead.

The girl looks in the glass.

Oh, how pretty you are. *(Kissing her passionately)*
GIRL *(Seriously)*: Keep on fixing the curl.
SERVANT *(As she combs)*: Happy girl, about to hold a man in
your arms, to kiss him, to feel his weight on your
body!
GIRL: Hush!
SERVANT: And the best thing of all is when you wake up
with him at your side, and feel his breath on your
shoulders—just like the feathers of a nightingale.
GIRL *(Loudly)*: Can't you just keep quiet?
SERVANT: But, child, what is a wedding, after all? A
wedding's just that and nothing more. Is it a cake? Is
it a bouquet of flowers? No. It's a shining bed, and a
man and a woman!
GIRL: You shouldn't say so.
SERVANT: That's something else again. But it's a mighty
fine thing!
GIRL: Or mighty bitter.
SERVANT: The orange blossoms I'm going to put here, right
here, so that they look like a crown on your hair. *(She
tries on the wreath of orange blossoms)*
GIRL *(Looking in glass)*: Give it to me. *(She takes the wreath,
looks at it and drops her hand)*
SERVANT: What's wrong?
GIRL: Leave me alone.
SERVANT: This is no time to be sad. *(Lively)* Give me the
orange blossoms.

The girl throws the wreath away.

Child! You're looking for bad luck, throwing your wreath away like that. Lift up your head! Don't you want to get married? Then say so! There's still time to refuse.

GIRL *(Rising)*: Just a passing cloud. I'll get over it.

SERVANT: You like your sweetheart, don't you?

GIRL: I like him.

SERVANT: I'm sure you do.

GIRL: But it's such a big step!

SERVANT: It's one you've got to take.

GIRL: Now that I've given my promise.

SERVANT: I'll put the crown on your head.

GIRL *(Sitting down again)*: Hurry up then. They ought to be here soon.

SERVANT: They've been on the way for at least two hours.

GIRL: How far is it from here to the church?

SERVANT: Five leagues along the river, and double that on the road.

As the girl gets up, the servant grows ecstatic seeing her.

The bride awakes
on her wedding morn,
and all the rivers of the world
come bringing her a crown.

GIRL *(Smiling)*: You're teasing me!

SERVANT *(Kissing her heartily and dancing about)*:
Awake with a green branch
of flowering laurel.

Awake with the branches
and trunks of the laurel!

Loud knocks on the doorknocker.

GIRL: Open the door. It must be the first guests. *(She exits)*
SERVANT *(Opening the door. Surprised)*: You?
LEONARDO: It's me! Good morning!
SERVANT: You're certainly the first to arrive.
LEONARDO: Wasn't I invited?
SERVANT: You were.
LEONARDO: Then that's why I came.
SERVANT: And your wife?
LEONARDO: I came on horseback. She's coming along the
    road.
SERVANT: Did you pass anyone?
LEONARDO: I left them way behind, on my horse.
SERVANT: You're going to kill that creature, running him
    like that.
LEONARDO: Well, when he's dead, he's dead! *(Pause)*
SERVANT: Sit down. Nobody's up yet.
LEONARDO: And the bride?
SERVANT: I'm just going to dress her now.
LEONARDO: The bride! She ought to be happy!
SERVANT *(Changing the conversation)*: How's the baby?
LEONARDO: What baby?
SERVANT: Your son?
LEONARDO *(As though dreaming)*: Oh!
SERVANT: Are they bringing him along?
LEONARDO: No.

There is a pause. Singing is heard in the distance.

VOICES:
> The bride awakes
> on her wedding morn.

LEONARDO:
> The bride awakes
> on her wedding morn.

SERVANT: The folks are coming. But they're still a long ways off.

LEONARDO: The bride will wear a big wreath, won't she? But it shouldn't be too big. A smaller one would be better for her. And say, has the groom brought the orange blossoms yet for her to put on her breast?

GIRL *(Entering. Still in petticoats with the wreath of orange blossoms on her head)*: He brought them.

SERVANT *(Loudly)*: Child, what's this?

GIRL: What does it matter? Why do you ask if he brought the orange blossoms? What do you mean by that?

LEONARDO: Nothing. What did you think I meant? *(Approaching)* You know *I* didn't bring them. Say! What have I meant to you anyway? Think back a little. But two oxen and a lousy shack weren't worth a thing! That's what hurts.

GIRL: What did you come here for?

LEONARDO: To see your wedding.

GIRL: I saw yours, too.

LEONARDO: Made by you. Tied by your two hands, yet even if I'm killed, no one will spit on me. But money, that glitters and shines, that can be like spit, too, sometimes.

GIRL: Liar!

LEONARDO: I'd better shut up. I'm a man with blood run-

ning in my veins, and I don't want those hills to know
what I have to say.

GIRL: I can say a lot more than you.

SERVANT: This kind of talk has got to stop. You mustn't
keep the past stirred up like that. *(She glances anxiously
at the door)*

GIRL: You're right! I shouldn't even speak to you. The
nerve of you! Coming here to see me now, getting in
the way of my wedding, insinuating about my orange
blossoms. Get out! And wait for your wife at the
door.

LEONARDO: You and I can't even talk together?

SERVANT *(Angrily)*: No, you can't talk together!

LEONARDO: After my own wedding, I wondered day and
night who was to blame. And every time I started to
think, a new blame came along and ate up the other
one. But somebody was to blame!

GIRL: There's a certain man with a horse who knows a lot,
and can do a lot to hurt a girl in the desert. But I'm
proud! That's why I'm getting married. And I'll lock
myself up with my husband, and it'll be my duty to
love him more than anybody else on earth.

LEONARDO *(Drawing near)*: Pride won't do you any good.

GIRL: Don't touch me!

LEONARDO: Just to stay quiet and burn up inside, that's the
worst thing that can happen to us. What good did
pride do me, keeping me away from you? Letting you
toss without sleep night after night? No good! It just
set me on fire inside, that's all! If you think time
heals, and walls shut out, it's not true. When something's deep down in your soul, there's nothing on
earth can tear it out!

GIRL *(Trembling)*: I can't listen to you! Oh, I can't bear to
hear your voice! It's just as if I'd drunk a whole bottle

of anisette and gone to sleep in a bed of roses. The
current drags me down, and I know I am drowning,
but I have to go.

SERVANT *(Grabbing Leonardo by the lapels)*: You've got to get
out! Now!

LEONARDO: This is the last time I'll ever have to talk to
her. Don't be afraid.

GIRL: I know I'm mad, and all torn up inside from what
I've had to bear, yet here I stand listening to you,
watching you lift your arms.

LEONARDO: I'd never have any peace if I didn't tell you
these things. I married! Now it's your turn.

SERVANT: And she'll marry, too!

VOICES *(Singing nearby)*:
   The bride awakes
   on her wedding morn.

GIRL: The bride awakes! *(She exits running)*

SERVANT: The folks are here. *(To Leonardo)* Don't go near
her again.

LEONARDO: Don't worry.

He exits left. The day dawns.

FIRST MAIDEN *(Entering)*:
   The bride awakes
   on her wedding morn.
   The night patrol passes
   and on each balcony there's a wreath.

VOICES:
   The bride awakes.

SERVANT *(Moving in the merry noise of the crowd)*:
Wake her with the green branch
of love in flower.
Wake her with the trunk
and the branches of the laurel.

SECOND MAIDEN *(Entering)*:
Wake her with long hair,
and a road of snow,
and patent-leather shoes,
and silver and jasmine
on her forehead.

SERVANT:
Oh, shepherdess,
The moon is rising!

FIRST YOUTH *(Enters waving his hat)*:
The bride awakes.
The wedding guests are coming
bringing trays full of flowers
and cakes for the feast.

VOICES:
The bride awakes.

SECOND MAIDEN:
The bride put on her white crown,
and the groom tied it
with golden ribbons.

SERVANT:
In her bed of sweet herbs
the bride cannot sleep.

THIRD MAIDEN:
> In the orange grove
> the groom has a knife and a napkin.

Three guests enter.

FIRST YOUTH:
> Awaken, little dove,
> for the dawn clears the sky
> of the bells of darkness.

GUEST:
> The bride! Fair bride!
> Today a maiden, tomorrow a woman.

FIRST MAIDEN:
> Come down, dark-haired girl,
> with your train of silk.

GUEST:
> Come down, little girl,
> to greet the dew of the morning.

FIRST YOUTH:
> Wake up, woman, wake up!
> For the breeze rains orange blossoms.

SERVANT:
> And a tree longs to deck itself
> full of red ribbons.
> On each ribbon is love
> with "long live" all around it.

VOICES:
> The bride awakes!

FIRST YOUTH:
> On her wedding morn!

GUEST:
> On her wedding morn,
> like a lady you are!
> Flower of the mountains,
> like the wife of a captain.

FATHER *(Entering)*:
> The groom carries off
> the wife of a captain.
> For a gift, he comes
> with his oxen.

THIRD MAIDEN:
> The groom is like a golden blossom.
> When he walks, little carnations
> gather in his footsteps.

SERVANT: Oh, happy girl!
SECOND YOUTH: The bride awakes!
SERVANT: Oh, little lady!
FIRST MAIDEN: The wedding feast beckons at all the windows.
SECOND MAIDEN: Bride, come out!
FIRST MAIDEN: Come out! Come out!
SERVANT: Let the bells ring! Clang and ring!
FIRST YOUTH: Here she comes! Here she comes!
SERVANT: Like a bull, the wedding feast comes to life!

> *The girl enters, in a black gown of the style of 1900, with*
> *a bustle and a long train of flowing gauze and stiff laces.*

Resting on her head is the crown of orange blossoms.
Guitars sound. The maidens kiss the bride.

THIRD MAIDEN: What kind of perfume have you got in your
hair?

GIRL *(Laughing)*: None.

SECOND MAIDEN *(Inspecting the dress)*: There's no cloth like
this anymore.

SECOND YOUTH: Hail to the groom!

BOY: Hail!

FIRST MAIDEN *(Putting a flower behind her ear)*: The groom is
like a golden blossom!

SECOND MAIDEN: What gentle glances in his eyes!

The boy and girl meet.

GIRL: Why did you wear those shoes?

BOY: They're gayer than the black ones.

WIFE *(Entering and kissing the girl)*: Hail!

All talk merrily at once. Leonardo enters solemnly, as
though performing a duty.

LEONARDO: A flower for your crown on your wedding
morn!

WIFE: Let the earth breathe in the fragrance of your hair!

MOTHER *(To the father)*: They're here, too?

FATHER: They're part of the family. Today's a day of
forgiveness.

MOTHER: I'll bear it, but I won't forgive.

BOY: Crowned with happiness, my darling!

GIRL: Let's go quickly to the church.

BOY: You're in a hurry?

GIRL: Yes! I want to be your wife—and stay with you
    alone—and never hear any other voice but your voice.

BOY: That's what I want, too.

GIRL: And never see any other eyes but your eyes. And
    have you hold me so tightly that even if my dead
    mother called me, I couldn't get away.

BOY: I've got two good strong arms. I'm going to hug you
    for forty years to come.

GIRL *(Dramatically, seizing his arm)*: No! Forever!

FATHER: Let's go! Get your horses! In your carts! The sun
    is up!

MOTHER: Be careful! We don't want any bad luck today.

The big doors at the rear open, and they all begin to exit.

SERVANT *(Crying)*: When you leave your house, sweet
    maiden, you leave like a star.

FIRST MAIDEN: Clean body, clean clothes, when you leave
    your house for the wedding.

SECOND MAIDEN *(As they go out)*: When you leave your
    house for the church . . .

SERVANT: The breeze strews flowers on the way.

THIRD MAIDEN: Oh, fair young girl!

SERVANT: Dark mist is the lace of your mantilla!

*They exit. Guitars, castanets and tambourines are heard.
Leonardo and the wife are left alone.*

WIFE: Come on.

LEONARDO: Where?

WIFE: To the church. But not on horseback. You're coming
    with me.

LEONARDO: In the wagon?

WIFE: What else is there?

LEONARDO: I'm not a man for riding in wagons.

WIFE: And I'm not a woman for going to weddings without my husband! I can't stand any more!

LEONARDO: I can't either!

WIFE: Why do you look at me like that? Your eyes are sharp as thorns.

LEONARDO: Let's go.

WIFE: I don't know what's come over you. But I think I know. And I don't want to think like that! But I realize this—you've finished with me. But I have a son. And another child coming. The same fate overtook my mother. Well, let's go. But I won't move a step without you.

VOICES *(Without)*:
> When you leave your home afar,
> You go to church like
> the morning star.

WIFE *(Crying)*: You go to church like the morning star! I went like that, too, out of my house. And all the countryside was at my wedding.

LEONARDO *(Rising)*: Come on!

WIFE: But with me!

LEONARDO: Yes, with you! Come on!

> *They exit.*
> *Curtain.*

SCENE TWO

*Outside the house of the bride. Landscape in tones of gray whites
and cold blues. Big fig trees. Shades of solemn silver. Panorama
of earth-colored mesas, all hard as a plaque in ceramics.*
   The servant is placing trays and glasses on a table.

SERVANT:
>   The wheel went round and round,
>   and the water went over,
>   and the wedding day came
>   when the branches parted
>   and the moon adorned herself
>   at her white railing.

>   *(Loudly)*
>   Put out the napkins!

>   The bride and groom sang and sang,
>   and the water went over,
>   and the wedding day came
>   that makes the frost sparkle
>   and fills with sweet honey
>   the bitter, bitter almonds.

>   *(Loudly)*
>   Bring out the wine!

>   Lady, lady, lovely lady!
>   Look how the water goes over—
>   for your wedding day's come
>   to gather in your train
>   and snuggle under your husband's wing

and stay in your house forever.
Your groom's like a male dove
with a heart of live coals,
and the whole countryside
waits for the blood.
The wheel goes round and round,
and the water goes over,
and the wedding day comes,
and the shining water!

MOTHER *(Entering)*: At last!

FATHER: Are we the first to get back?

SERVANT: No. Leonardo came a while back with his wife, racing like the wind. The woman was half-dead with fright. They made it so fast they must have come on horseback.

FATHER: That boy's looking for trouble. He's not a good sort.

MOTHER: How is he ever going to amount to anything? All his folks are the same. It's handed down from his great-grandfather who started out killing, and it runs through all their bad breed. Knife-slingers and folks with a false smile!

FATHER: Well, let's not talk about it.

SERVANT: Why not talk about it?

MOTHER: It hurts me to the very roots of my veins. Like a mark on all of them, the only thing I can see is the hand that killed my men. Look at me here! Do I look like I'm crazy? If I am, it's because I've never been able to cry as loud as my heart wants to. Always ready to burst out, this cry I have to grab and smother with my two hands. But then when they bring in the dead, I have to keep quiet. People talk.

FATHER: Today's not the time to think about such things.

MOTHER: When I think about it, I have to talk. And today, more than ever. For today, I'll be alone in my house.

FATHER: But waiting for company.

MOTHER: That's what I'm hoping for—grandchildren.

They sit down.

FATHER: I hope they have plenty of children. We need hands for these fields that don't have to be paid, for there's always war with these weeds and thistles and stones that spring up from God knows where! And those hands must belong to us owners who are willing to sweat and worry over the land until the seeds spring up. The land needs a great many sons.

MOTHER: And a daughter or so too! Boys belong to the wind. They have to carry arms. But girls, they never run the streets.

FATHER *(Happily)*: I guess they'll have both boys and girls.

MOTHER: My son is wild about her. And he's a real man! His father could have had a great many sons by me.

FATHER: I wish it could happen in a day. Right away, they'd have two or three full-grown men!

MOTHER: But it isn't like that. It takes a long time. That's why it's so terrible to see the blood of any one of them spilled on the ground. A red fountain that runs only a moment, costs us years. That day when I got to my son, he had fallen in the middle of the street. I wet my hands in his blood and licked them with my tongue—because he was mine. You don't know what it means! The earth drank up that blood that I would have put in an urn of crystal and topaz.

FATHER: Now, you'll just have to wait. My daughter is able, and your son is strong.

MOTHER: I hope so. *(She rises)*
FATHER: Get the bowls of hot cereal ready.
SERVANT: They're ready.

The wife enters, followed by Leonardo.

WIFE: Congratulations!
MOTHER: Thank you.
LEONARDO: Is there going to be a party?
FATHER: Not much. The people can't stay.
SERVANT: Here they come!

Guests enter in lively groups. The bride and groom come arm in arm. Leonardo exits.

BOY: I never saw so many people at a wedding.
GIRL *(Solemnly)*: Never.
FATHER: It was fine!
MOTHER: Whole flocks of relations came.
BOY: People that never leave their houses.
MOTHER: Your father sowed good seed and now you live to reap it.
BOY: There were cousins of mine I never knew I had.
MOTHER: All our kinfolks from the coast.
BOY *(Gaily)*: The horses got scared. *(He talks on to others)*
MOTHER *(To the bride)*: And what are you thinking?
GIRL: Nothing.
MOTHER: Congratulations are tiresome.

Guitars are heard playing.

GIRL: Awfully tiresome.
MOTHER: But they shouldn't be. You ought to be light as a dove.

GIRL: Are you spending the night with us?

MOTHER: No. No one's at home.

GIRL: But you ought to stay.

FATHER *(To the mother)*: Look at the dance they're dancing. A dance from the seacoast.

Leonardo comes out and sits down. His wife stands rigid behind him.

MOTHER: They're my husband's cousins, firm as rocks when it comes to dancing.

FATHER: I like to watch them. What changes have come over this house today! *(He exits toward the dancing)*

BOY *(To his bride)*: Do you like the orange blossoms?

GIRL *(Staring straight ahead of her)*: Yes.

BOY: They're all of wax, so they'll last forever. I wish you could have had them all over your dress.

GIRL: What for?

Leonardo exits right.

FIRST MAIDEN: Let's go take the pins out.

GIRL *(To her husband)*: I'll be right back.

The girl and maiden exit.

WIFE: I hope you'll be happy with my cousin.

BOY: I'm sure I will be.

WIFE: Both of you here together, never having to go away, making a happy home. I wish I lived far away from everything, like this.

BOY: Why don't you buy some land? It's cheap up on the hills, and better to bring up children.

WIFE: We haven't any money! And the way things are going
    now!

BOY: Your husband's a good worker.

WIFE: Yes, but he likes to jump from one thing to another
    too much. He's not a steady sort of man.

SERVANT: Won't you have something to eat? I'm going to
    wrap up some wine-cakes for your mother. She likes
    them a lot.

BOY: Sure, give her three dozen.

WIFE: No, no! A half-dozen's enough.

BOY: A holiday's a holiday!

WIFE *(To the servant)*: Where is Leonardo?

SERVANT: I haven't seen him.

BOY: He must be down there with the rest of the folks.

WIFE: I'm going to look. *(Exits)*

SERVANT: Pretty sight, isn't it?

BOY: But you're not dancing!

SERVANT: Nobody's asked me.

Two guests cross in the background. Until the end of the
scene, there is a gay crossing and recrossing of figures.

BOY *(Merrily)*: That's funny! Lively old girls like you dance
    better than the young ones.

SERVANT: Stop throwing bouquets at me, boy! Such folks,
    your family! Men among men! When I was a girl, I
    was at your grandfather's wedding. What a man! He
    was just like a mountain getting married!

BOY: I'm not as big as all that.

SERVANT: No, but there's the same look in your eyes!
    Where's the bride?

BOY: Taking off her headdress.

SERVANT: Oh! Well, look! Since you won't be asleep at

midnight, I've fixed you some ham, and two big glasses of ripe old wine, down there in the bottom part of the closet, if you want it.

BOY *(Grinning)*: I won't be eating at midnight.

SERVANT *(Slyly)*: If not you, then the bride. *(Exits)*

FIRST YOUTH *(Entering)*: You've got to have a drink with us.

BOY: I'm waiting for the bride.

SECOND YOUTH: You'll see her in the wee hours of the morning.

FIRST YOUTH: That's the best time!

SECOND YOUTH: Come along!

BOY: Let's go.

They exit. Shouts and happy cries. The girl enters. From the opposite side, two maidens come running to meet her.

FIRST MAIDEN: Who did you give the first pin to, to her or to me?

GIRL: I don't remember.

FIRST MAIDEN: You gave it to me, right here.

SECOND MAIDEN: No, no! She gave it to me in front of the altar.

GIRL *(Worried and troubled within)*: I tell you, I don't know.

FIRST MAIDEN: But I wanted you to . . .

GIRL *(Rudely)*: I don't care! I've got something else to think about.

SECOND MAIDEN: Oh! I'm sorry.

Leonardo crosses in the background.

GIRL *(Seeing Leonardo)*: It's a hard hour for me.

FIRST MAIDEN: We don't know about that.

GIRL: You'll know when the time comes. This is a step that means a lot.

FIRST MAIDEN: But are you upset about something?

GIRL: No. Forgive me.

SECOND MAIDEN: For what? But either of the two pins will bring us husbands, won't they?

GIRL: Either of them.

FIRST MAIDEN: But one of us will get married before the other.

GIRL: Are you as anxious as all that?

SECOND MAIDEN *(Blushing)*: Yes.

GIRL: Why?

FIRST MAIDEN: Because . . .

Embracing, the two maidens run away. The boy enters. The girl does not see him. Very slowly, from behind, he puts his arms around her.

GIRL *(Jumping violently)*: Get away!

BOY: You're afraid of me?

GIRL: Oh! It's you?

BOY: Why, who else could it be? *(Pause)* Your father or me.

GIRL: You're right.

BOY: But your father wouldn't have hugged you so hard.

GIRL: Hardly!

BOY: He's too old. *(He hugs her a little brusquely)*

GIRL *(Dully)*: Leave me alone.

BOY *(Releasing her)*: Why?

GIRL: Because, the people . . . they can see us.

The servant crosses in the background without looking at the lovers.

BOY: What of it? Now it's holy.

GIRL: Yes, but let me alone! Later.

BOY: What's the matter? Are you afraid?

GIRL: Nothing's the matter. Don't go.

The wife of Leonardo enters.

WIFE: I'm sorry to bother you, but . . .
BOY: What is it?
WIFE: Did my husband come past here?
BOY: No.
WIFE: I can't find him. And his horse isn't in the barn.
BOY *(Gaily)*: He must be giving it a run.

The wife exits anxiously. The servant enters.

SERVANT: Aren't you happy about so much to-do?
BOY: But I wish they'd get it over with now. My wife here's
      a little tired.
SERVANT: What's the matter, child?
GIRL: I feel like something's beating at my temples.
SERVANT: A bride out of these mountains ought to be
      strong. *(To the boy)* You're the only one that can cure
      her, since she's yours. *(Exits running)*
BOY *(Caressing her)*: Let's go dance awhile. *(He kisses her)*
GIRL *(In anguish)*: No. I want to lie down a little.
BOY: I'll keep you company.
GIRL: Never!! With all these people here? What would they
      say? Let me be quiet a minute or two.
BOY: If you want to. But don't act like that tonight.
GIRL *(At the door)*: Tonight I'll feel better.

She exits.

BOY: That's what I'll be waiting for.
MOTHER *(Entering)*: Son?
BOY: Where've you been?

MOTHER: Down there with the crowd. Are you happy?

BOY: Yes!

MOTHER: Where's your wife?

BOY: Resting a little. It's a hard day for a bride.

MOTHER: Hard day? It's the best day. For me it was like coming into a fortune.

The servant enters and goes towards the girl's room.

It's the breaking of new ground, the planting of new trees.

BOY: You're leaving?

MOTHER: Yes, I have to be at home.

BOY: Alone?

MOTHER: Alone, no. My head is full of things, of men, and of fights.

BOY: But fights that are over now.

The servant enters running rapidly toward the rear.

MOTHER: As long as we live, we fight.

BOY: I'll always listen to you.

MOTHER: Try to always be loving to your wife. And if sometimes she's touchy and mean, pet her in a way that hurts her a little, a big hug, a bite—and then a gentle kiss after that. Not enough to make her angry, but enough to let her know that you're a man, the master, and the one that runs things. That's what I learned from your father. But since he isn't here, I'm the one who'll have to tell you what the secrets of being a man are.

BOY: I'll always do as you tell me.

FATHER *(Entering)*: Where's my daughter?

BOY: In the house.

FIRST MAIDEN: Come on, you newlyweds, we're going to dance a reel.

FIRST YOUTH *(To the groom)*: You'll call the figures!

FATHER *(Coming out)*: But she isn't there!

BOY: No?

FATHER: Maybe she went up on the balcony.

BOY: I'll go see.

He enters the house. Laughter and guitars are heard.

FIRST MAIDEN: The dance is starting. *(Exits)*

BOY *(Coming out)*: She's not there either.

MOTHER *(Worried)*: No?

FATHER: Then where could she have gone?

SERVANT *(Entering)*: My child, where is she?

MOTHER *(Solemnly)*: We don't know.

The boy exits. Three guests enter.

FATHER: Isn't she down there dancing?

SERVANT: She's not down there dancing.

FATHER *(An outburst)*: There's a lot of people down there! Go look!

SERVANT: I did look.

FATHER *(Tragically)*: Then where is she?

BOY *(Returning)*: No luck! She's nowhere around.

MOTHER *(To the father)*: What *is* this? Where is your daughter?

Suddenly the wife of Leonardo enters.

WIFE: They've gone! They've gone! She and Leonardo! On horseback, wrapped in each other's arms, like the wind!

FATHER: It's not true! My daughter, no!

MOTHER: Your daughter, yes! The offshoot of a bad mother. And him—him, too! Yes, him! But she's already my son's wife.

BOY: Let's go get them! Who has a horse?

MOTHER: Who has a horse? Now! Right now! Who has a horse? I'll give all I've got, my eyes, my tongue . . .

VOICE: Here's a horse!

MOTHER *(To her son)*: Go on! Get them!

He exits with the two youths.

No, don't go! They'll kill quickly and surely. . . . But yes, run! And I'll follow!

FATHER: It couldn't be her. Maybe she drowned herself in the cistern.

MOTHER: Good girls drown themselves, clean girls! Not that one! But she's my son's wife now. And there are two camps! Two camps here!

All gather around to hear.

My family and yours. Let's get out of here and wipe this dust from our feet. We'll go help my son!

The crowd divides into two groups.

For he has help on his side, my son! All his cousins from the sea, and all those from inland. Be off! Down all the roads. The day of blood has come again. Two camps! You with yours, and I with mine! Follow me! Follow me!

Curtain.

Act Three

SCENE ONE

A wood. Night. Great moist tree trunks. Gloom. Violins playing in the distance. Three woodcutters enter.

FIRST WOODCUTTER: Have they found them?

SECOND WOODCUTTER: No, but they're looking for them everywhere.

THIRD WOODCUTTER: They'll come across them.

SECOND WOODCUTTER: Sh-sss-ss-s!

THIRD WOODCUTTER: What is it?

SECOND WOODCUTTER: Seems like they're coming down all the roads at once.

FIRST WOODCUTTER: We can see them when the moon comes out.

SECOND WOODCUTTER: They'd better let them alone.

FIRST WOODCUTTER: Yes, the world is wide. There's room for everybody.

THIRD WOODCUTTER: But they're going to kill them.

SECOND WOODCUTTER: Since they had to do what they did, they were wise to run away.

FIRST WOODCUTTER: They kept on trying to fool each other, but their blood got the best of them.

THIRD WOODCUTTER: Their blood!

FIRST WOODCUTTER: You've got to do what your blood tells you.

SECOND WOODCUTTER: But the very blood the sun warms, the earth drinks up.

FIRST WOODCUTTER: So what? Better be dead with the blood flowing, than live with it rotting within.

THIRD WOODCUTTER: Shut up!

FIRST WOODCUTTER: What? Do you hear something?

THIRD WOODCUTTER: I hear the crickets, the frogs, all the lurking noises of the night.

FIRST WOODCUTTER: You don't hear a horse?

THIRD WOODCUTTER: No.

FIRST WOODCUTTER: Now he must be loving her.

SECOND WOODCUTTER: Her body meant for him, and his body meant for her.

THIRD WOODCUTTER: But they'll find them and kill them.

FIRST WOODCUTTER: By then, they'll have mingled their blood, and they'll be like two empty vessels, like two dry streams.

SECOND WOODCUTTER: There're plenty of clouds. Maybe the moon won't come out.

THIRD WOODCUTTER: The husband will find them, moon or no moon. I saw him leave like an angry star, his face the color of ashes. Wearing the mark of destiny— the destiny of his breed.

FIRST WOODCUTTER: Breed that dies in the middle of the street.

SECOND WOODCUTTER: You're right.

THIRD WOODCUTTER: Do you think they can break the spell?

SECOND WOODCUTTER: That's hard to say. For ten leagues, all around now, there are knives and guns.

THIRD WOODCUTTER: He rides a good horse.

SECOND WOODCUTTER: But there's a woman with him.

FIRST WOODCUTTER: Well, we're just about where we're going.

SECOND WOODCUTTER: There's that tree with forty limbs. We'll chop it down directly.

THIRD WOODCUTTER: The moon's coming out. Let's hurry.

Light floods in from the left.

FIRST WOODCUTTER: Oh, rising moon! Moon of the big leaves!

SECOND WOODCUTTER: Covered with jasmine blossoms of blood.

FIRST WOODCUTTER: Oh, lonely moon! Moon of the green leaves!

SECOND WOODCUTTER: Silver on the face of the bride.

THIRD WOODCUTTER: Wicked moon, leave a dark bower somewhere for the lovers.

FIRST WOODCUTTER: Oh, sad, sad moon! Leave a dark bower for the lovers.

They exit. In the glow at the left the moon appears. The moon is a young woodcutter with a white face. The whole scene is a brilliant blue.

MOON

A white swan in the river,
eye of the cathedrals,
false dawn on the leaves am I.
They can't get away from me!
Who tries to hide?

Who's sobbing in a thicket
in the valley?
The moon leaves a knife
hanging in the air,
lurking steel for the pain of blood.
Let me in! I'm frozen
on walls and windows!
Open tile roofs and breasts
where I can get warm!
I am cold! My ashes
of sleepy metals
seek a crest of flames
in the mountains and the streets.
I carry snow on my
shoulders of jasper,
and the water of the ponds
pours over me, cold and hard.
But tonight, I will have
cheeks red with blood,
and reeds will gather
at the feet of air.
There's no shade and no ambush
where they can escape me!
I need to hide in some breast
somewhere to warm me.
A heart for me! A warm heart
flowing from the mountains
of my breast.
Let me in! Oh, let me in!

(To the trees)
I want no shade. My rays
must go everywhere,
so through your dark trunks

let there be streaks of light,
so that tonight I may have
my cheeks sweet with blood,
and the reeds gathered
at the feet of the air.
Who's hiding! Out, I say!
No! There's no escape!
I'll make your horse glitter
like a fever of diamonds.

The moon disappears among the trees, and the scene is dark again. An old woman, a beggar, comes out all covered with gray-green rags. She is barefoot. You can hardly see her face for the rags. She is not a part of the company.

BEGGAR: The moon is gone, and they are on their way here. But they'll never pass. The whisper of the river'll smother in the whisper of the trees the broken flight of their cries. It'll happen here, and soon. I'm tired. Open your trunks and let white rays fall on the floor of the bedrooms where heavy bodies lie with wounds at their throats. Not a bird need awake. And the breeze'll gather their cries in her skirts and fly with them over the black mountains, or bury them somewhere in soft linen. *(Impatiently)* Oh, that moon! That moon!

The moon enters in a flood of blue light.

MOON: They're coming. Some up the glen and others by the river. I'm going to light up even the stones. What do you need?

BEGGAR: Nothing.

MOON: The air is hardening, like a two-edged knife.

BEGGAR: Light up their vests and unbutton their buttons, so that the knives will find the way.

MOON: But they'll take a long time dying. And the blood will make a soft sound in my fingers. Look how my hollows of ash awaken, anxious for the trembling of that spouting fountain.

BEGGAR: We won't let them pass that stream there! . . . Silence!

MOON: There they come!

He exits. The scene is dark.

BEGGAR: Hurry! Light! Plenty of light! You hear me? They can't get away!

The boy enters with the first youth. The beggar sits down, covering herself with a mantle.

BOY: Along about here!

FIRST YOUTH: You won't find them.

BOY *(Forcefully)*: I will find them.

FIRST YOUTH: I think they've taken another direction.

BOY: No. I heard his horse's gallop a moment ago.

FIRST YOUTH: It might be another horse.

BOY: Listen! There's only one horse in the world, and it's that horse. Understand? If you come with me, come without talking.

FIRST YOUTH: I only want to . . .

BOY: Shut up! I'm sure I'll find them here. You see this hand? Well, it's not my hand. It's the hand of my brother, and of my father, and of all our family that are dead. And it's so strong I could tear out that tree by the roots if I wanted to. But let's go on, for I feel all my family's teeth gritting so tight it's hard for me to breathe.

BEGGAR *(Moaning)*: Ah!

FIRST YOUTH: Did you hear that?

BOY: Go on and look around.

FIRST YOUTH: This is a hunt.

BOY: A hunt! The best hunt of all!

The youth exits. The boy goes rapidly toward the light and comes upon the beggar. She is Death.

BEGGAR: Ah-h-h!

BOY: What do you want?

BEGGAR: I'm cold.

BOY: Where are you going?

BEGGAR *(Always whining like a beggar)*: Away off...

BOY: Where did you come from?

BEGGAR: Over there, a long ways.

BOY: Did you see a man and a woman go by on horseback?

BEGGAR *(Suddenly alive)*: Wait! *(She looks at him)* A good-looking boy! *(She rises)* But much better looking, if you were asleep—

BOY: Listen! Answer me! Did you see them?

BEGGAR: Wait! What broad shoulders you have! How would you like to be stretched out on those broad shoulders, and not have to walk on the narrow soles of your feet?

BOY *(Shaking her)*: I asked you, did you see them? Did they come by here?

BEGGAR: They didn't. But they're coming down the hill now. Don't you hear them?

BOY: No.

BEGGAR: Don't you know the road?

BOY: I'll find it, no matter what it's like.

BEGGAR: I'll go with you. I know the way.

BOY *(Impatiently)*: Then let's go! Which way?

BEGGAR: That way!

> *They exit quickly. Two violins in the distance sing like the singing of the woods. The woodcutters return with their axes on their shoulders. They walk slowly among the trees.*

FIRST WOODCUTTER: Oh, Death arising! Death of the big leaves!

SECOND WOODCUTTER: Don't open your gates of blood.

FIRST WOODCUTTER: Oh, lonely Death! Death of the dry leaves!

THIRD WOODCUTTER: Don't cover their wedding with your flowers.

SECOND WOODCUTTER: Oh, sad, sad Death! Leave a green branch for love!

FIRST WOODCUTTER: Oh, wicked Death! Leave a green branch for love!

> *They exit speaking. Enter Leonardo and the girl.*

LEONARDO: Keep still!

GIRL: From here on, I'll go alone. Go back! I want you to go back!

LEONARDO: Keep quiet, I said.

GIRL: Take your teeth, take your hands, take whatever you can and break this chain of purity about my neck, and throw me in a corner there in a cave. And if you don't kill me like a little serpent, then give me the mouth of your gun in my hands. Oh, what pain! What

fire flames in my head! What splinters of glass stick to
my tongue!

LEONARDO: We've done it now! Be quiet. They're after us,
near, and I've got to keep you with me.

GIRL: Then you'll have to make me stay with you.

LEONARDO: Make you stay? Who came down the steps
first?

GIRL: I came down first.

LEONARDO: Who put the reins on the horse?

GIRL: I did. You're right.

LEONARDO: And whose hands put the spurs on my feet?

GIRL: My hands that are your hands. But when I look at
you, they want to break the blue and whispering
branches of your veins. I love you! I love you! Leave
me here! If I could kill you, I'd make you a shroud
out of petals of violets. Oh, what pain, what fire
flames in my head!

LEONARDO: What splinters of glass stick to my tongue! I
tried to forget. And I put a wall of stone between your
house and my house. Didn't I? You remember. And
when I saw you far off, I threw sand in my eyes. But
when I got on my horse, the horse went to your door.
Needles of silver turned my blood black, and in my
sleep dark weeds grew in my body. It's not my fault.
It's the fault of the earth, and the sweet scent your
hair, and the sweet scent of your breasts.

GIRL: Oh, how foolish we all are! I don't want to share
your bed, nor your food, yet there isn't a minute in
the whole day I don't want to be with you. If you call
me, I'll come. If you told me to fly, I'd follow you
through the air like a bit of grass in the wind. I've left
a good man and all his offspring, in the midst of the
wedding feast, with my orange blossoms on. But

you'll suffer for it! And I don't want you to suffer.
Leave me here alone. Fly! Get away! There's nobody
left to help you.

LEONARDO: The birds of dawn are swaying in the trees,
and night is dying on the sharp edges of the stones.
Let's go off in some dark place where I've always
wanted you. We don't have to care what people say
now, nor what ugly poisons they spread. *(He embraces
her passionately)*

GIRL: I'll lay at your feet, watching over your dreams.
Naked, at your feet like a dog, watching all around.
When I look at you, your beauty burns me, consumes
me.

LEONARDO: Fire burns fire! One little flame can kill two
spikes of grain. Let's go! *(He pulls her after him)*

GIRL: Where are you dragging me?

LEONARDO: Where these men who are after us can't come.
Where I can look at you forever.

GIRL *(Sarcastically)*: Then drag me from fair to fair, the
shame of all good women, and let people see me, with
the sheets of my wedding bed flying like flags!

LEONARDO: If I thought as people should think, I'd want to
leave you. But I'm going where you go. And you're
going with me. Take one step, and I'll prove it! Nails
of moonlight bind your hips to mine.

The whole scene is violent and full of great sensuousness.

GIRL: Listen!

LEONARDO: Someone's coming!

GIRL: Run! It's right for me to die here, with my feet in the
water and thorns on my head. The leaves will weep
for me, a lost woman, still virgin.

LEONARDO: Be quiet! They're coming.

GIRL: Run! Run!

LEONARDO: Be still! So they won't hear us. Go ahead!
Let's go, I said!

She wavers.

GIRL: Yes, both together!

LEONARDO *(Embracing her)*: Death alone can part us.

GIRL: Then I'll die, too.

> *They exit in each other's arms. Slowly, the moon comes
> out. The wood is flooded with a brilliant blue light. Two
> violins are heard. Suddenly, two long shrieks split the
> night and cut short the music of the violins. At the second
> cry, the beggar appears and remains with her back turned.
> She opens her shawl and stands there like a huge bird
> with enormous wings. The moon stands still. Silence.*
> *Curtain.*

SCENE TWO

*A white room with thick arches and thick walls. At the right and
left, white stairways. A thick high arch at the back in a wall of
white. The floor is also a shining white. The room is simple but
monumental, like a church. There is no gray, no shadow, not
even enough for perspective.*

Two girls dressed in blue are unwinding a red skein of wool.

FIRST MAIDEN:
Skein of wool, skein of wool,
what would you like to be?

SECOND MAIDEN:

> A flower of a dress
> or the crystal of a paper.
> To be born at four
> and then die at ten.
> Just a skein of wool,
> a chain on his feet,
> and a knot that binds
> the bitter laurel.

CHILD *(Singing)*:

> Didn't you go to the wedding?

FIRST MAIDEN: No.

CHILD: I didn't either. What could have happened under the vines in the vineyard? What happened among the olive trees? What happened that nobody's come back yet? Didn't you go to the wedding?

SECOND MAIDEN: We told you *no*.

CHILD *(Starting out)*: I didn't either.

SECOND MAIDEN:

> Skein of wool, skein of wool,
> what do you want to sing?

FIRST MAIDEN:

> Wounds of wax and pain of myrtle.
> Sleep in the morning to wake at night.

CHILD *(At the door)*:

> Skein of wool strikes the flint.
> Blue mountain lets them pass.
> Run, run, run, and after awhile

you'll run into a knife and
need no more bread.

She exits.

SECOND MAIDEN:
Skein of wool, skein of wool,
what do you say?

FIRST MAIDEN:
Stretched out forever
by the river's gloom,
a speechless lover,
and a crimson groom.

They pause and look at the skein.

CHILD *(Appearing in the doorway)*: Run! Run! Run! Bring
the skein here! I see them coming, covered with mud.
Two bodies stretched out on sheets of marble!

*She exits. The wife and mother-in-law of Leonardo
appear. They are torn by anguish.*

FIRST MAIDEN: Are they coming?
MOTHER-IN-LAW *(Shortly)*: We don't know.
SECOND MAIDEN: Tell us about the wedding.
FIRST MAIDEN: Yes, tell us.
MOTHER-IN-LAW *(Drily)*: There's nothing to tell.
WIFE: I want to go back and find out everything.
MOTHER-IN-LAW *(Positively)*: You, you go home. Brave and
alone at home, you'll grow old and weep with the
door closed. Never again, dead or alive. We'll nail up

the windows, and let night and the rain cover the
bitter weeds.

WIFE: What could have happened?

MOTHER-IN-LAW: It doesn't matter. Put a veil on your face.
Your sons are your own and no one else's. Put a cross
of cinders over your bed where his pillow was.

They exit.

BEGGAR *(At the door)*: Bread, little girls, a piece of bread.

CHILD *(Running in front of her)*: Make her get away!

The girls gather near each other.

BEGGAR: Why?

CHILD: Because you whine. Get away!

FIRST MAIDEN: Child!

BEGGAR: I *could* ask for your eyes. A cloud of black birds
follow me. Do you want one?

CHILD: I want you to go away.

SECOND MAIDEN *(To the beggar)*: Pay her no mind.

FIRST MAIDEN: Did you come by way of the river?

BEGGAR: That's the way I came.

FIRST MAIDEN *(Timidly)*: Could we ask you something?

BEGGAR: I saw them! They'll be here directly. Two torrents
of water calm at last among the big rocks. Two men
under the horse's feet, dead in the beautiful night.
(With savory pleasure) Dead! Yes, dead!

FIRST MAIDEN: Hush, you old woman, you! Hush!

BEGGAR: Their eyes are broken flowers and their teeth two
handfuls of hard snow. Both of them went down,
while the bride fled with blood on her dress and
blood on her hair. Now, covered with two sheets

they'll come, born on the shoulders of tall young men.
That's all that happened. It was due to happen.
Muddy sand on the golden flower. Muddy sand on
the golden flower.

*She exits. The maidens hang their heads and walk out in
rhythm, repeating her words.*

FIRST MAIDEN: Muddy sand...
SECOND MAIDEN: ...on the golden flower.
CHILD: On a golden flower they bring the lovers from the
stream. Dark brown the one, and dark brown the
other. A nightingale of darkness sobs flying over the
golden flower!

*They exit. The room is empty. The mother enters with her
neighbor. The neighbor is crying.*

MOTHER: Hush, now.
NEIGHBOR: I can't.
MOTHER: Hush, I say. *(At the door)* Anyone here? *(She puts
her hands to her head)* My son ought to answer me.
But my son is nothing but an armful of dry flowers
now. My son, just a dark voice in the mountains.
(Angrily to the neighbor) Can't you keep quiet? I don't
want tears in this house. Your tears come from the
eyes, that's all. But when I'm alone, mine come from
the soles of my feet and the roots of my hair. They
burn like blood.
NEIGHBOR: Come over to my house. Don't stay here.
MOTHER: I want to stay here. And quietly, now they're all
dead. At midnight I'll go to sleep, and sleep without
being frightened anymore by pistols or knives. Other

mothers will stand at their windows, whipped by the rain, watching for their sons to come home. Not I. I'll make sleep a dove of cool marble carrying frosty camellias to the cemetery. But no! No graveyard. No! Just a bed of earth that shelters them and rocks them underneath the sky.

A woman in black enters and kneels down at the right.

(To the neighbor) Take your hands down from your face. Terrible days are coming. I don't want company. The earth and I. Just my grief and I. And these four walls. Oh! Oh-oo-o! *(She sits down, rigid)*

NEIGHBOR: Have pity on yourself.

MOTHER *(Pushing her hair back)*: Yes, I must be calm. The neighbors are coming and they mustn't see me so poorly! So poor! A woman without a single son to hold to her bosom.

The girl enters in a black shawl. She no longer wears her orange blossoms.

NEIGHBOR *(Looking angrily at the girl)*: Where are you going?

GIRL: I'm coming here.

MOTHER *(To the neighbor)*: Who is that?

NEIGHBOR: Don't you know her?

MOTHER: That's why I ask, who is she. I have to keep from knowing her, not to drive my teeth into her throat. You snake! *(She rushes threateningly toward the girl, then stops. To her neighbor)* You see her there crying? And me standing calmly here without tearing her eyes out! I don't understand myself. Is it that I didn't love my

son? But what about his own honor? Where is his
honor?

She strikes the girl, knocking her to the floor.

NEIGHBOR: Lord have mercy! *(Tries to separate them)*
GIRL *(To the neighbor)*: Leave her alone. I came so they
    could kill me, and carry me away with the others. *(To
    the mother)* But not with your hands. With a fork, with
    a sickle, hard, until my bones break. Let her alone. I
    want her to know that I'm clean! I may be mad, but
    I'll go to my grave with no man ever having looked
    upon the whiteness of my breasts.
MOTHER: Shut up! Shut up! What's that to me?
GIRL: Because I went with him. Yes, I went. *(In anguish)*
    You would have gone, too. I was like a woman on
    fire, covered with burns inside and out. And your son
    was like cool water to give me children and land and
    make me well again. But that other one, he was a
    great dark river with a song in his teeth, and the
    whisper of reeds, and branches. I needed your son
    who was like cool water, a little boy of water. But that
    other one came like a flock of wild birds so thick I
    couldn't move. And they covered my burning flesh
    with hoarfrost, the flesh of a poor young girl, caressed
    in the arms of flame. I didn't want to! Listen! Listen
    to me! I say I didn't want to! Listen! Listen! I didn't
    want him! Your son was my destiny, and I never
    deceived him. But the arms of that other one, they
    tore me away like a wave of the sea, like a stubborn
    mule taking the lead! And they would have torn me
    away always, always, even if I had been an old woman
    with all your son's sons holding me by the hair!

Another neighbor-woman enters.

MOTHER *(Sarcastically)*: You're not guilty, and I'm not guilty! Who is guilty, then? Lazy, spoiled, sleepless woman throwing away her orange blossoms for the edge of a bed some other woman's made warm!

GIRL: Don't say that! Take your revenge! Here I am! My throat is soft, as easy as cutting a flower in your garden. But don't say that! No! I'm clean, clean as a newborn babe. And I am strong enough to prove it. Light the fire! We'll put our hands in it. You, for your son. And me, for my body. You'll take yours out first!

Enters another neighbor.

MOTHER: What do I care about your purity? What do I care about your dying? What does it matter to me, anyway? Bless the grain because my sons rest beneath it. Bless the rain because it wets the faces of the dead. Bless God who will lay us all down to rest together.

GIRL: Let me weep with you.

MOTHER: Weep, but there at the door.

The child enters. The girl remains in the doorway. The mother is in the center of the room. The wife enters and goes to the left.

WIFE: He was a good horseman, and now he's a mountain of snow. He rode to the fairs, to the mountains, and to the arms of women. Now, foam of darkness crowns his brow.

MOTHER: Sunflower of his mother! Looking glass of earth!

Put on his breast a cross of bitter oleanders. Cover
him with a sheet of shining silk. And let the water
form a pool of tears in your still hands.

WIFE: Oh! Four men are coming with tired shoulders!

GIRL: Oh! Four young men are carrying death through the
air!

MOTHER: My neighbors.

CHILD *(At the door)*: There they come, bringing them.

MOTHER: Always the same! The cross.... The cross.

GIRL: May the cross shelter the dead and the living!

MOTHER: Friends! With a knife, one day with a knife, between two and three, two men in love killed each
other. With a knife, with a little knife almost too small
to hold in your hand, but sharp to find its way
through startled flesh to stop entangled in the trembling roots of a cry!

GIRL: A knife, a little knife almost too small to hold in your
hand, a fish with no scales out of water. One day,
between two and three, with this knife two men,
stretched out rigid forever, with their lips turned yellow.

MOTHER: And it's almost too small to hold in your hand,
but sharp to find its way through startled flesh to stop
entangled in the trembling roots of a cry.

The neighbors kneel on the floor and weep.
Curtain.

Yerma

TRANSLATED BY
W. S. MERWIN

CHARACTERS

Yerma

Juan

Maria

Victor

First Old Woman

Girl 1

Girl 2

Six Washerwomen

First Sister-in-Law

Second Sister-in-Law

Old Woman 1

Old Woman 2

Dolores

Woman 1

Woman 2

Male Figure

Female Figure

Child

Man 1

Man 2

Man 3

Act One

SCENE ONE

As the curtain rises, Yerma is discovered asleep, with a work-basket at her feet. The stage is filled with a strange dreamy light. A shepherd enters on tiptoe, keeping his eyes fixed on Yerma. He is leading by the hand a child dressed in white. The clock strikes. When the shepherd leaves, the lights changes to the cheerful light of a spring morning. Yerma wakes.

SONG
> *(A voice within)*
> For baby, for baby,
> We'll make, for baby,
> A little nest in the field,
> And we'll get inside.

YERMA: Juan. Are you there? Juan.
JUAN: I'm coming.
YERMA: It's time.
JUAN: Have the oxen gone past?
YERMA: Yes they have.

JUAN: Goodbye. *(He starts out)*

YERMA: Don't you want some milk?

JUAN: What for?

YERMA: You work hard and you're not built for it.

JUAN: It's the thin ones that are like steel.

YERMA: Not you. You weren't like that when we were married. Your face has got all white as though you never had it in the sun. I'd rather you went down to the river and went swimming, and went up onto the roof when the rain was lashing the house. Twenty-four months we've been married and all the time you've got thinner and thinner as though you were growing backwards.

JUAN: Anything else?

YERMA *(Getting up)*: Don't get angry. If I were sick I'd like it if you took care of me. "My wife's not well. I'll butcher that sheep and make her a nice stew. My wife's not well. I'll save that chicken fat for her cough; I'll get the sheepskin to keep the snow off her feet." That's what I'd do. So I look after you.

JUAN: Thank you.

YERMA: But you don't let me.

JUAN: There's nothing the matter with me. You've just made it up. I work hard. Every year I'll be older.

YERMA: Every year . . . you and I will go on living here, every year . . .

JUAN *(Smiling)*: Naturally. And in peace and quiet. The work's going well, and we've got no children to cost us money.

YERMA: We've got no children . . . Juan!

JUAN: What?

YERMA: Don't I love you?

JUAN: I don't say that.

YERMA: I know girls that shook and sobbed before getting into bed with their husbands. Did I cry before I
went to bed with you the first time? Didn't I sing as I
lifted the sheets of embroidered linen? Didn't I say to
you, "The bedclothes smell like apples"?

JUAN: That's what you said.

YERMA: My mother cried because I wasn't sad to leave her.
It was true! Nobody was ever so happy to get married.
But just the same . . .

JUAN: Be quiet. It's bad enough having to listen all the
time to . . .

YERMA: No. Don't tell me what they say. I can see with my
own eyes that there's something the matter. . . . Even
when it falls on the stones the rain softens them
enough for the hedge mustard to grow up on them,
that people say is good for nothing. "That hedge
mustard's good for nothing." But I watch it waving its
yellow flowers when there's a breath of wind.

JUAN: Well, don't give up.

YERMA: I won't. *(She throws her arms around him and kisses
him, taking the initiative herself)*

JUAN: If you need anything tell me and I'll bring it. You
know I don't like you going out.

YERMA: I never go out.

JUAN: You're much better here.

YERMA: Yes.

JUAN: The street is for people with nothing to do.

YERMA *(Downcast)*: Of course.

*The husband goes out and Yerma turns to the workbasket.
She passes her hand over her waist, raises her arms in a
beautiful yawn and sits down to sew.*

(Sings)
Where do you come from, my love, my baby?
"From the height of the hard cold."
What do you lack, my love, my baby?
"The warm cloth you're wearing."

(She threads her needle)
Let the branches wave at the sun
And the fountains leap up all around.

(As though talking to a baby)
The dog barks in the courtyard.
The wind sings in the trees.
The oxen low in the cow byre
And the wind ruffles my hair.
What are you asking for, my baby,
From so far away?

(Pause)

"The white hills of your breasts."
Let the branches wave at the sun
And the fountains leap up all around.

(Sewing)
It's true what I tell you, my baby,
I'm cut and broken for you.
Now the belt at my waist hurts me
That will be your first cradle!
When will you come, my baby?

(Pause)

"When your body smells of jasmine."
Let the branches wave at the sun
And the fountains leap up all around.

Yerma goes on singing. Maria comes in through the doorway, carrying a bundle of clothes.

Where've you been?
MARIA: To the store.
YERMA: So early?
MARIA: I'd have liked to be waiting at the door when they opened. You know what I've bought?
YERMA: Coffee for breakfast, sugar, bread.
MARIA: No. I bought lace, and three skeins of yarns, and ribbons, and colored wool to make pompoms. With money from my husband; he gave it to me himself.
YERMA: You're going to make a blouse.
MARIA: No, it's because . . . can't you tell?
YERMA: What?
MARIA: Because it's here!

She stands with her head lowered. Yerma stands and looks at her admiringly.

YERMA: After five months!
MARIA: Yes.
YERMA: You could tell?
MARIA: Naturally.
YERMA *(Curious)*: What does it feel like?
MARIA: I don't know. I'm afraid.
YERMA: Afraid. *(Holding her)* But . . . when did you know it was there? . . . Tell me. You weren't expecting it.

MARIA: No, I wasn't.

YERMA: You were singing, weren't you? I keep singing. And you . . . tell me.

MARIA: Don't ask me. Didn't you ever hold a live bird in your hand?

YERMA: Yes.

MARIA: Well, like that . . . but in your blood, inside it.

YERMA: How beautiful! *(She gazes at Maria excitedly)*

MARIA: I'm in a daze. I don't know anything.

YERMA: About what?

MARIA: What I should do. I'll ask my mother.

YERMA: What for? She's old, she'll have forgotten everything about it. Don't walk around too much, and when you breathe breathe as softly as though you had a rose between your teeth.

MARIA: Listen. They say that later he gives little kicks.

YERMA: And that's when you love him most, when you can start saying, "My baby."

MARIA: And at the same time it makes me feel shy.

YERMA: What's your husband said?

MARIA: Nothing.

YERMA: Does he love you very much?

MARIA: He never says so. But when he comes near me his eyes tremble like two green leaves.

YERMA: Did he know that you . . . ?

MARIA: Yes.

YERMA: How did he know?

MARIA: I don't know. But on our wedding night he whispered to me all the time with his mouth against my cheek, so that to me it's as though my baby is a dove of light that he had slipped into my ear.

YERMA: How lucky you are!

MARIA: But you know more about all that than I do.

YERMA: What good does it do me?

MARIA: That's true. But why? Of all the girls that were married about that time you're the only one . . .

YERMA: That's how it is. Oh, there's still time. Elena was three years, and some of the old ones, back in the time of my mother, took much longer than that, but just the same, two years and twenty days, like me, it's too long. I don't think it's right that I should waste away here. At night I often go out into the patio, barefoot, to walk on the earth, I don't know why. If it goes on like this I'll end up sick.

MARIA: Don't be silly, girl. To hear you talk you'd think you were an old woman. Now listen! Nobody has any right to complain about these things. One of my mother's sisters didn't have her first until after fourteen years, and you should see what a beautiful little boy it is.

YERMA *(Anxiously)*: What was he like?

MARIA: He cried like a little bull, as loud as a thousand locusts all singing at once, and he wet all over us and pulled our hair, and when he was only four months old he scratched our faces all to pieces.

YERMA *(Laughing)*: But those things don't hurt.

MARIA: I tell you . . .

YERMA: Bah! I've seen my sister nurse her baby when her breast was a mass of scars, and it hurt her terribly, but it was a cool pain, and a good one, the kind you need for your health.

MARIA: They say babies hurt very much.

YERMA: It's a lie. It's the weak mothers that say that, the whimperers. Why do they have them, then? Having a baby isn't like having a bunch of roses. We have to suffer to be able to see them grow. I believe that half of our blood must go into them. But that's good, and sound, and beautiful. Every woman has enough blood for four or five babies and if she doesn't have them it turns to poison. That's what's going to happen to me.

MARIA: I don't know what I feel.

YERMA: I always heard that the ones that were having their first were afraid.

MARIA *(Timid)*: Maybe.... You're so good at sewing...

YERMA *(Taking the bundle)*: Give me that. I'll cut out the baby clothes. And what's this?

MARIA: They're the swaddling clothes.

YERMA: Very well. *(She sits down)*

MARIA: Well... then I'll see you soon.

Maria approaches Yerma, who seizes her belly lovingly.

YERMA: Don't walk on the rough places in the street.

MARIA: Goodbye. *(She kisses Yerma and goes)*

YERMA: Come back soon.

Yerma resumes her position from the beginning of the scene. She takes up the scissors and starts to cut. Victor enters.

Good morning, Victor.

VICTOR *(Thoughtful, determined and grave)*: Where's Juan?

YERMA: In the field.

VICTOR: What are you sewing?

YERMA: I'm cutting out swaddling clothes.

VICTOR *(Smiling)*: Well!

YERMA *(Laughing)*: I'll put lace on the hems.

VICTOR: If it's a girl you can name her after you.

YERMA *(Trembling)*: What...?

VICTOR: I'm happy for you.

YERMA *(Half choking)*: They're not . . . not for me. They're for Maria's baby.

VICTOR: Good; well, maybe you'll follow her example. There ought to be a baby in this house.

YERMA *(With anguish)*: Ought to be!

VICTOR: Well, do something about it. Tell your husband to think less about work. He wants to get some money together and he will, but who's he going to leave it to when he dies? I'm off with the sheep. Tell Juan to get the two he bought from me, and as for the other one, tell him to plough deeper. *(He goes out smiling)*

YERMA *(Sings)*:

> That's it, plough deeper!
> It's true what I tell you, my baby,
> I'm cut and broken for you.
> How the belt at my waist hurts me
> That will be your first cradle!
> When will you come, my baby?
> "When your body smells of jasmine!"

Yerma gets up and goes to where Victor had been standing and breathes deeply, as though breathing in mountain air; then she goes to the other side of the room as though looking for something, turns and comes back and sits down again and takes up her sewing. She starts to sew and remains with her eyes on her stitching.

> *Curtain.*

SCENE TWO

In the fields. Enter Yerma, carrying a basket. The first old woman enters.

YERMA: Good day.

FIRST OLD WOMAN: And to you, girl. Where are you going?

YERMA: I've taken his meal to my husband, over there in the olives.

FIRST OLD WOMAN: Have you been married long?

YERMA: Three years.

FIRST OLD WOMAN: Any children?

YERMA: No.

FIRST OLD WOMAN: Bah! You will.

YERMA *(Anxiously)*: Do you think so?

FIRST OLD WOMAN: Why not? *(She sits down)*
I've taken my husband his meal too. He's old. He still works. I've got nine sons like suns in the sky, but I've got no daughter, so I still have to do the fetching and carrying.

YERMA: You live on the other side of the river.

FIRST OLD WOMAN: That's right. There at the mills. What family are you from?

YERMA: I'm Enrique the shepherd's daughter.

FIRST OLD WOMAN: Oh, Enrique the shepherd. I knew him. Good people. Get up. Sweat. Eat a little bread. Die. No play, nothing like that. Holidays are for other people. Silent. Silent. I could have married your uncle. But oh, I was one for whirling the skirts; off like an arrow for the melons, the fiestas, the sugar cakes. Many's the morning I peeped out of the door in the small hours thinking I heard guitars coming and going, but it was only the breeze. *(Laughs)*
You'll laugh at me. I've had two husbands, fourteen

children, five of them died, but I got over it. I'd like
to live a long, long time. Because what I say is: Look
how old the fig trees get, and how long the houses go
on standing, and it's only as devilish old women that
collapse into dust at nothing at all.

YERMA: I want to ask you something.

FIRST OLD WOMAN: Let me look. *(She looks at Yerma)* I
know what you're going to say. There's nothing to say
about those things. *(She gets up)*

YERMA *(Holding her back)*: Why not? Listening to you has
given me hope. I've been wanting for a long time to
talk with an old woman. Because I want to find out.
Yes. You'll tell me . . .

FIRST OLD WOMAN: What?

YERMA *(Lowering her voice)*: What you know. Why haven't
I had any? Am I supposed to devote all the best of my
life to feeding hens or hanging starched curtains in
my window? No. You have to tell me what I must do,
and I'll do it whatever it is, even if you tell me to stick
needles into the softest part of my eyes.

FIRST OLD WOMAN: Me? I don't know anything. I turned
up my mouth and started singing. Babies arrive like
water. Oh, nobody could say you don't have a
beautiful body. You take a step and the stallion
whinnies at the end of the street. Oh, let me be, girl,
don't ask me to talk. I think many things that I don't
want to say.

YERMA: Why? With my husband I never talk of anything
else.

FIRST OLD WOMAN: Listen. Do you care for your husband?

YERMA: What do you mean?

FIRST OLD WOMAN: Do you love him? Do you want him?
Do you want to be with him . . . ?

YERMA: I don't know.

FIRST OLD WOMAN: Don't you tremble when he comes near you? Don't you feel as though you were in a dream when he brings his lips near you. Tell me.

YERMA: No. I never felt that.

FIRST OLD WOMAN: Never? Not even when you've been dancing?

YERMA *(Remembering)*: Maybe.... Once.... Victor...

FIRST OLD WOMAN: Well?

YERMA: He caught me around the waist and I couldn't say anything to him because I couldn't speak. Another time when I was fourteen the same one, Victor, (he was big by then) picked me up in his arms to jump over a ditch and I started shivering so hard my teeth rattled. But I was always shy.

FIRST OLD WOMAN: And with your husband?

YERMA: My husband's different. My father chose him for me, and I agreed. I was glad to. That's the truth. And the first day I was betrothed to him I had already started thinking...about babies.... And I looked at myself in his eyes. Yes I did, but it was only so that I could see myself as a tiny little girl, very good and obedient, as though I were my own daughter.

FIRST OLD WOMAN: It wasn't like that with me. Maybe that's why you haven't had any babies yet. Men have to be something you like, girl. We have to want them to undo our hair and give us their mouths to drink like water. That's how the world is.

YERMA: Yours, not mine. I imagine many things, many things, and I'm sure my son will accomplish them all. It was for him that I gave myself to my husband, and it's to be able to have him that I go on giving myself to my husband, it's not for my own pleasure.

FIRST OLD WOMAN: And so you stay empty.

YERMA: Empty? No, I'm not empty. There's something growing in me, but it's hate. Tell me, is it my fault? Do we have to hope for nothing from a man but himself? If that's all, what can you think about when he leaves you there with your sad eyes staring at the ceiling, and turns over and goes to sleep? Am I supposed to go on thinking about him, or about the wonderful thing that might come out of me? I don't know. *(She kneels)* Have pity on me. Tell me!

FIRST OLD WOMAN: Oh, what an open flower! What a beautiful creature you are! Go away. Don't make me say any more. I don't want to talk to you anymore. They're matters of honor, these things, and I don't burn anyone's honor. Find out for yourself. You really shouldn't be quite so innocent.

YERMA *(Sadly)*: Girls that grew up in the country like I did find all the doors closed. It's never anything but hints and winks, because they say you can't know anything about all that. You too, you won't say anything either, and you'll go away looking wise and knowing all about it, but refusing to give any to somebody who's dying of thirst.

FIRST OLD WOMAN: I'd talk to a sensible woman. Not to you. I'm old, and I know what I'm saying.

YERMA: Then God help me.

FIRST OLD WOMAN: Not God. I never cared much for God. When are you going to wake up and see there isn't any? It's men that have to help you.

YERMA: But why do you say that to me? Why?

FIRST OLD WOMAN *(Going)*: Just the same there ought to be a God, but only a little one, to strike down the men with the rotten seed who muddy up the happiness of the fields.

YERMA: I don't know what you mean.

FIRST OLD WOMAN: That's all right. I do. Don't be down-hearted. Go on hoping; don't stop. You're still young. What do you want me to do?

The old woman goes. Two girls appear.

GIRL 1: There seem to be people everywhere.

YERMA: The men are working in the olive groves. We have to take them their meals. Nobody's at home but the old people.

GIRL 2: Are you going back to the village?

YERMA: I'm going that way.

GIRL 1: I have to hurry. I left the baby asleep and nobody in the house.

YERMA: Well, run, girl! You can't leave babies alone. Do you keep pigs at your place?

GIRL 1: No. But you're right. I'll hurry.

YERMA: Go on. That's how things happen. I suppose you left the door shut.

GIRL 1: Naturally.

YERMA: Yes, but you don't realize what babies are like. The least little thing and that's the end of them. A little needle, a swallow of water.

GIRL 1: You're right. I'll run. I hadn't thought of that.

YERMA: Go on.

GIRL 2: If you had four or five you wouldn't talk that way.

YERMA: Why not? Even if I had forty.

GIRL 2: Anyway, things are more peaceful for you and me without any.

YERMA: Not for me.

GIRL 2: Well, they are for me. What a worry! And there's my mother, never stops giving me herbs to take so

that I'll have one, and in October we're going to the
shrine where they say you can get one if you ask for
one hard enough. My mother's going to ask for one.
Not me.

YERMA: Why did you get married?

GIRL 2: Because they married me. Everybody gets married.
If we go on like this the only ones that won't be
married will be the children. Well, and besides . . . you
really get married a long time before you go to the
church. But the old women put their noses into
everything. I'm nineteen and I don't like cooking and
washing. Well, so all day I have to do what I don't
like. What for? Why does my husband have to be my
husband? Just because we did what all the other
betrothed couples do these days. Old wives'
stupidities!

YERMA: Be still. Don't say things like that.

GIRL 2: You'll call me crazy too, crazy, crazy! *(She laughs)*
I can tell you the only thing I've learned in my life:
Everybody's shut up in their houses doing what they
don't like. It's better out in the street. I go down to
the stream, I go up and ring the bells, I have a cool
drink of anis.

YERMA: You're a child.

GIRL 2: Maybe, but I'm not crazy. *(She laughs)*

YERMA: Does your mother live in the house at the top of
the village?

GIRL 2: Yes.

YERMA: The last house?

GIRL 2: Yes.

YERMA: What's her name?

GIRL 2: Dolores. Why do you ask?

YERMA: No reason.

GIRL 2: Why do you want to know?

YERMA: Who knows?...I heard...

GIRL 2: Well, it's your business....Look, I'm going to take
my husband his meal. *(She laughs)* Pity I can't say my
boyfriend, eh? *(She laughs)* So much for crazy, see?
(She starts off, laughing happily) Goodbye.

VICTOR *(Off, sings)*:
Why sleep alone, shepherd?
Why sleep alone, shepherd?
On my wool bed cover
You'd sleep better.
Why sleep alone, shepherd?

Yerma listens.

Why sleep alone, shepherd?
On my wool bed cover
You'd sleep better.
Your coverlet of dark stone,
    shepherd,
And your shirt of frost,
    shepherd,
Gray winter bulrushes
In the night of your bed.
The oaks lay needles,
    shepherd,
Under your pillow,
    shepherd,
And if you hear a woman's voice
It's the broken voice of the water.
    Shepherd, shepherd.

What does the mountain want of you,
> shepherd?
Mountain of bitter grasses,
What baby is killing you?
The thorn of the broom.

She starts out and meets Victor, entering.

VICTOR *(Happily)*: Where are you going, my beauty?

YERMA: Were you singing?

VICTOR: Yes, it was me.

YERMA: How beautiful. I never heard you before.

VICTOR: No?

YERMA: What strength in your voice! Like a jet of water
that fills your whole mouth.

VICTOR: I'm happy.

YERMA: It's true.

VICTOR: The same way that you're unhappy.

YERMA: It's not so much that I'm unhappy as that I've
reason to be.

VICTOR: And your husband's more unhappy than you are.

YERMA: Oh yes. It's his nature. Dry.

VICTOR: He always was.

Pause. Yerma sits down.

Have you brought him his meal?

YERMA: Yes. *(She looks at him. Pause)* What have you got
there? *(She points at his face)*

VICTOR: Where?

YERMA *(Getting up and going over to Victor)*: There ... on
your cheek; like a burn.

VICTOR: Nothing.

YERMA: I thought it was something.

Pause.

VICTOR: It must be the sun.
YERMA: Perhaps.

Pause. The silence grows more pronounced, and, without the slightest gesture, a struggle begins between the two characters.

(Trembling) Listen.
VICTOR: What?
YERMA: Didn't you hear crying?
VICTOR *(Listening)*: No.
YERMA: I thought I heard a baby crying.
VICTOR: Yes?
YERMA: Quite near. As though it couldn't get its breath.
VICTOR: There are a lot of children around here that come to steal fruit.
YERMA: No. It was the voice of a little baby.

Pause.

VICTOR: I didn't hear anything.
YERMA: It must have been something I imagined.

She looks at him fixedly. Victor returns the look, then looks aside slowly, as though afraid. Juan enters.

JUAN: What are you still doing here?
YERMA: Talking.
VICTOR: Keep well. *(He goes)*

JUAN: You should be at the house.

YERMA: I was enjoying myself.

JUAN: I can't think what you were doing.

YERMA: I was listening to the birds.

JUAN: Well. That's how people start talking.

YERMA *(With energy)*: Juan. What do you mean?

JUAN: It's not me. It's what people will say.

YERMA: People can go to the devil!

JUAN: Don't curse. It's ugly in a woman.

YERMA: If only I were a woman.

JUAN: That's enough. Go to the house.

Pause.

YERMA: Well. Will you be coming?

JUAN: No. I'll be up at the watering ditches all night. There's only a little water running and it's mine until sunrise, and I have to stay and watch out for water thieves. Go to bed and sleep.

YERMA *(Dramatically)*: I'll sleep!

Curtain.

Act Two

SCENE ONE

Singing can be heard before the curtain rises. A torrent in which the village women are washing clothes. The washerwomen are at different levels.

WASHERWOMEN:
> In the cold stream
> I'm washing your sash.
> Your laugh is like
> A jasmine burning.

WASHERWOMAN 1: I don't like gossip.

WASHERWOMAN 3: Everybody gossips here.

WASHERWOMAN 4: I don't see any harm in it.

WASHERWOMAN 5: If people want a good reputation they should look after it.

WASHERWOMAN 4:
> I planted a sprig of thyme
> And I watched it grow.

If you care for a good name
Watch what you do.

They laugh.

WASHERWOMAN 5: That's what they say.

WASHERWOMAN 1: But you can't be sure.

WASHERWOMAN 4: Well, we do know that the husband's brought both his sisters to live with them.

WASHERWOMAN 5: The old maids?

WASHERWOMAN 4: Yes. They used to look after the church and now they'll look after their sister-in-law. I couldn't live with those two.

WASHERWOMAN 1: Why not?

WASHERWOMAN 4: I'd be afraid to. They're like those big leaves that grow all of a sudden on graves. They're covered with wax. They're all turned in on themselves. They make me think they must cook their meals in lamp oil.

WASHERWOMAN 3: Have they moved in yet?

WASHERWOMAN 4: Yesterday. The husband's going back out to his fields again.

WASHERWOMAN 1: But does anybody know what happened?

WASHERWOMAN 5: The night before last, cold as it was, she spent the whole night sitting out on the doorsill.

WASHERWOMAN 1: But why?

WASHERWOMAN 4: She hates being in her own house.

Pause.

WASHERWOMAN 5: Those women that don't have babies get like that. When they ought to be making lace and apple preserves they take a fancy to go up onto the roof, or to walk barefoot in the river.

WASHERWOMAN 1: Who are you to say things like that? It's not her fault she doesn't have any children.

WASHERWOMAN 4: The women that want them get them. Your lazy Janes and your momma's girls and your kiss-me-dainties aren't going to see their bellies get wrinkled.

They laugh.

WASHERWOMAN 3: And they daub themselves with white powder and red powder and pick little bunches of oleander and go after somebody who's not their husband.

WASHERWOMAN 5: That's the sacred truth!

Pause.

WASHERWOMAN 1: But have any of you ever seen her with anybody else?

WASHERWOMAN 4: We haven't but other people have.

WASHERWOMAN 1: It's always other people!

WASHERWOMAN 5: Twice, they said.

WASHERWOMAN 2: And what were they doing?

WASHERWOMAN 4: Talking.

WASHERWOMAN 1: That's no sin.

Pause.

WASHERWOMAN 4: There's another thing in the world and that's how the eyes look. My mother always said so. A woman looking at roses isn't the same as a woman looking at the thighs of a man. It's the way she looks at him.

WASHERWOMAN 1 : At who?

WASHERWOMAN 4 : Somebody. *(Pause)* Understand? Find out for yourself, do you want me to say it louder?

Laughter from several of them.

And when she's not looking at him, because she's alone and doesn't have him in front of her, she's got a picture of him in her eyes.

WASHERWOMAN 1 : That's a lie!

Hubbub.

WASHERWOMAN 5 : And the husband?

WASHERWOMAN 3 : He might be deaf. Not even moving, like a lizard in the sun.

They laugh.

WASHERWOMAN 1 : It would all take care of itself if they had children.

WASHERWOMAN 2 : Those are all things that point to people whose fate's working against them.

WASHERWOMAN 4 : That house gets more like hell by the hour. She and her sisters-in-law whitewash the walls all day, and rub the copper and polish the glasses and oil the hearthstones, without ever opening their lips, and the more everything shines the hotter it gets.

WASHERWOMAN 1 : It's his fault. Any man who doesn't give his wife babies ought to look after her.

WASHERWOMAN 4 : It's her fault. She's got a tongue like a flint.

WASHERWOMAN 1: What devil's got into your hair to make you say things like that?

WASHERWOMAN 4: And who told you you could give me advice?

WASHERWOMAN 2: Stop it!

WASHERWOMAN 1: I'd like to string every gossiping tongue on a knitting needle.

WASHERWOMAN 2: That's enough!

WASHERWOMAN 4: And I'd like to smother the hypocrites.

WASHERWOMAN 2: Be still. Can't you see? The sisters-in-law.

Murmurs. Yerma's sisters-in-law enter. They are in mourning. They begin washing, in general silence. Sound of bells.

WASHERWOMAN 1: Are the shepherds going out already?

WASHERWOMAN 3: Yes, all the flocks are going out.

WASHERWOMAN 4 *(Taking a deep breath)*: I like the smell of sheep.

WASHERWOMAN 3: Yes?

WASHERWOMAN 4: Why not? It's the smell of something that belongs to you. And I like the smell of the red mud that the river's full of in the winter.

WASHERWOMAN 3: You and your fancies.

WASHERWOMAN 5: All the flocks are going out together.

WASHERWOMAN 4: It's a flood of wool. They sweep everything along with them. If the green wheat had a head it would tremble to see them coming.

WASHERWOMAN 3: Look how they run! What a band of enemies!

WASHERWOMAN 1: They're all out. Every one of them.

WASHERWOMAN 4: Let me see . . . no . . . no, there's one that's not there.

WASHERWOMAN 5: Which one?

WASHERWOMAN 4: Victor's.

The two sisters-in-law straighten up and look.

(Sings)
In the cold stream
I'm washing your sash.
Your laugh is like
A jasmine burning.
I want to live
In that flower's small
Snowfall.

WASHERWOMAN 1:
Oh the dry wife
With her breasts of sand!

WASHERWOMAN 5:
Tell me if your husband
Still has some seed
So that the water
Can sing through your blouse.

WASHERWOMAN 4:
Your shirt
Is a silver boat
And a wind on the shores.

WASHERWOMAN 1:
I've come to wash
My baby's clothes
To give the water
Lessons in crystal.

WASHERWOMAN 2:
Now my husband's coming
Up the mountain to eat.
He's bringing me a rose
And I have three for him.

WASHERWOMAN 5:
From the plain my husband
Came in to dinner.
The live coals he brings me
I cover with myrtle.

WASHERWOMAN 4:
My husband has come through the air
To sleep.
I am red village pinks
And he is of the same flower.

WASHERWOMAN 1:
Lay flower upon flower
When summer dries the tongue of the reaper.

WASHERWOMAN 4:
And open the bellies of dreamless birds
When winter calls at the door
Trembling.

WASHERWOMAN 1:
Groan between the sheet.

WASHERWOMAN 4:
And sing!

WASHERWOMAN 5:
> When your man brings us
> The crown and the bread.

WASHERWOMAN 4:
> So that the arms entwine.

WASHERWOMAN 2:
> So that the light breaks into our throats.

WASHERWOMAN 4:
> So that the wood softens in the branches.

WASHERWOMAN 1:
> And the tents of the wind cover the mountains.

WASHERWOMAN 6 *(Appearing at the top of the torrent)*:
> So that a baby
> Melts the brittle windows of the dawn.

WASHERWOMAN 1:
> And our bodies are filled
> With furious branches of coral.

WASHERWOMAN 6:
> So that there may be oarsmen
> On the waters of the sea.

WASHERWOMAN 1:
> A little baby, a baby.

WASHERWOMAN 2:
> And the doves open their wings and their bills.

WASHERWOMAN 3:
A baby crying, a son.

WASHERWOMAN 4:
And the Men step forward
Like wounded stags

WASHERWOMAN 5:
Joy, joy, joy
Of the belly swollen under the dress.

WASHERWOMAN 2:
Joy, joy, joy
Of the navel, the tender calyx of wonder.

WASHERWOMAN 1:
But oh the dry wife
The one with the breasts of sand!

WASHERWOMAN 3:
May light shine out of her!

WASHERWOMAN 4:
May she run!

WASHERWOMAN 5:
May light shine out of her again!

WASHERWOMAN 1:
May she sing!

WASHERWOMAN 2:
May she go into hiding!

WASHERWOMAN 1:
    May she sing again!

WASHERWOMAN 6:
    The dawn that my baby
    Brings in his garment.

WASHERWOMEN *(They sing in chorus)*:
    In the cold stream
    I'm washing your sash.
    Your laugh is like
    A jasmine burning.
    Ah! Ah! Ah!

    They move the clothes rhythmically, pounding them.
    Curtain.

SCENE TWO

Yerma's house. Near sundown. Juan is seated. The sisters-in-law are standing.

JUAN: You say she left only a little while ago?

The elder sister nods.

She must be at the fountain. But you know I don't like her to go out alone. *(Pause)* You can set the table.

The younger sister leaves.

I can tell you I've earned the bread I eat.

(To his sister) It was a hard day yesterday. I was pruning the apple trees and at the end of the afternoon I got to wondering why I worked so hard at it when I couldn't even lift an apple to my mouth. I'm tired. *(He passes his hand over his face. Pause)*

And she's not back.... One of you ought to go with her. That's what you're here for, eating from my board and drinking my wine. My life's in the fields, but my honor's here. And my honor is yours too.

The sister bows her head.

Don't take that wrong.

Yerma enters with two water jars. She stops in the doorway.

Have you been to the fountain?

YERMA: So there'd be cool water for supper.

The elder sister goes out.

How are the fields?
JUAN: I was pruning trees yesterday.

Yerma sets down the jars. Pause.

YERMA: Are you staying?
JUAN: I have to go watch the flocks. You know I have to. They're mine.
YERMA: I know. Don't go over it again.
JUAN: Every man has his own life to live.

YERMA: Every woman too. I'm not asking you to stay. I've got all I need here. Your sisters look after me very well. Fresh bread and farm cheese and roast lamb, that's what I have here. And your flocks on the mountain have grass with the dew on it. I think you can be at peace.

JUAN: To be at peace one's mind has to be at rest.

YERMA: And yours isn't.

JUAN: No.

YERMA: Think about something else.

JUAN: Haven't you learned yet what I'm like? The sheep in the sheepfold and the women in the house. You go out too much. I always said so, didn't you hear me?

YERMA: That's right. The women in their houses. When the houses aren't tombs. When the chairs get broken and the linen sheets wear out with use. It's not like that here. Every night when I go to bed I find the bed newer, brighter, as though it had just been brought back from the city.

JUAN: You know, yourself, that I have a right to complain. There are things I have to watch out for.

YERMA: What? I don't do anything that would offend you. I obey you in everything, and whatever I suffer I keep locked up in my own body. And every day will be worse. We won't say anything. I'll learn to bear my cross as well as I can, but don't ask me any questions. If I could only turn into an old woman right away, with a mouth like a shriveled flower, I'd be able to smile at you and manage quite well at living with you. But as it is, I'll bear it alone.

JUAN: I don't understand you, the way you talk. I don't deny you anything. I send to all the towns around for the things you like. I have my faults, but what I want

is peace and quiet with you. I want to be able to sleep
out there and know that you're sleeping too.

YERMA: But I don't sleep. I can't sleep.

JUAN: Is there anything you don't have? Tell me. Answer
me!

YERMA *(Deliberately, and looking steadily at her husband)*: Yes.

Pause.

JUAN: Always the same. Over five years now. I'd almost
forgotten.

YERMA: But I'm not you. Men have their own life, the
cattle, the trees, their conversations; but women don't
have anything else but that: having children, and
looking after them.

JUAN: Everybody isn't the same. Why don't you take one of
your brother's children? I don't mind.

YERMA: I don't want to look after other people's children. I
think my arms would freeze if I held them.

JUAN: So you drive yourself mad with this silly idea of
yours, instead of thinking of all the things you ought
to be doing. You insist on beating your head against a
stone.

YERMA: A stone that should be ashamed to be a stone.
That should be a basket of flowers. That should be
fresh water.

JUAN: There's nothing but restlessness and discontent all
around you. After all, you ought to resign yourself.

YERMA: I came inside these four walls not to resign myself.
When I have my head tied up in a handkerchief so
that I can't open my mouth, and my hands clamped
down in the coffin, then I'll have resigned myself.

JUAN: Well, what do you want to do?

YERMA: I want to drink water, and there's no glass and no water. I want to climb the mountain and I have no feet; I want to embroider my skirt and I haven't any thread.

JUAN: The trouble is that you aren't a real woman, and you're trying to ruin a man who hasn't any choice.

YERMA: I don't know what I am. Let me go out and talk about it, to let it come out. I haven't failed you in any way.

JUAN: I don't want people pointing me out. That's why I want to see that door shut, and everybody home where they belong.

The first sister enters slowly and goes to a cupboard.

YERMA: It's no sin talking to people.

JUAN: But it can look like one.

The second sister comes in, goes to the water jug and fills a pitcher.

I don't want any more of this. When you're told something keep your mouth shut and remember that you're a married woman.

YERMA *(With astonishment)*: Married!

JUAN: And that every family has its honor, which is a burden they all share.

The sister with the pitcher goes out slowly.

But it's there, dark and easy to break, flowing in our blood.

The other sister goes out carrying a platter, almost as though she were in a procession. Pause.

Forgive me.

Yerma looks at her husband. He raises his head, and his eyes meet hers.

From the way you look at me I shouldn't ask you to forgive me, I should force you, I should lock you in. That's why I'm your husband.

The two sisters appear in the doorway.

YERMA: Don't say anything about it. I beg you. Let it rest.

Pause.

JUAN: Let's go in and eat.

The sisters go in.

Did you hear me?
YERMA *(Gently)*: You go and eat with your sisters. I'm not hungry yet.
JUAN: As you like.

YERMA *(As though dreaming)*:
Oh what a field of torment!
Oh what a door closed upon misery!
I ask to suffer for a child and the air
Offers me dahlias of the sleeping moon.
These my two fountains of warm milk

Are, in the thickness of my flesh,
Two pulses of a horse's veins,
That thrash the branch of my anguish.

Oh breasts blind under my clothes!
Oh doves without eyes or whiteness!
Oh what pain of imprisoned blood
Is sticking wasps to my neck!
But you must come, my love, my baby,
For the water gives salt, the earth fruit,
And our womb bears tender children
As the cloud carries soft rain.

(She looks toward the door) Maria! Why do you hurry
past my door that way?

Maria enters with a baby in her arms.

MARIA: I always do when I've got the baby. Because it
    makes you cry.
YERMA: Yes. *(She takes the baby and sits down)*
MARIA: I'm sad that it makes you envious.
YERMA: I'm not envious. I'm poor.
MARIA: Don't be sad.
YERMA: How can I help but be sad when I see you and the
    other women filled with flowers inside, and then see
    how useless I am in the middle of so much happiness.
MARIA: But you have other things. If you'd listen to me you
    could be happy.
YERMA: A country woman who has no children is as useless
    as a bunch of thorns. She's even bad; I say it even
    though I'm one of those Godforsaken wretches
    myself.

Maria makes a move to take the baby away.

Take him. He likes it better when you hold him.
Probably I don't have mother's hands.

MARIA: Why do you say that to me?

YERMA *(Standing)*: Because I've had enough. Enough of
having hands and not being able to hold anything of
my own. Because I'm mortified. I'm mortified and I'm
lower than anything on earth, when you think that the
wheat comes up, the fountains give water endlessly,
and the sheep bear lambs by the hundreds, and the
bitches, and it's as though the whole countryside kept
standing up to show me the tender sleeping things
that it had borne, while I feel two blows of a hammer
here instead of my baby's mouth.

MARIA: I hate it when you talk like that.

YERMA: You women who have babies haven't any thought
for us who don't. You stay cool and ignorant. Just like
people who are swimming in fresh water can't think
what thirst is like.

MARIA: I always tell you the same thing. I don't want to say
it all again.

YERMA: Each time I want it more and I have less hope.

MARIA: Horrible.

YERMA: I'll end by believing that I'm my own child. Often
I go down to feed the oxen at night. I never did it
before. It's not a woman's job. And when I walk
through the dark in the shed my footsteps sound like
a man's.

MARIA: Everyone has to do things his own way.

YERMA: And in spite of everything he still wants me. You
see what my life is like!

MARIA: And your sisters-in-law?

YERMA: May you see me dead and unshrouded if ever I
    speak to them.
MARIA: And your husband?
YERMA: All three of them are against me.
MARIA: What's in their minds?
YERMA: Things they make up. About people who have
    guilty consciences. They imagine that I might be
    tempted by some other man, and they don't under-
    stand that even if I were, with my people honor
    comes before everything. They're stones in front of
    me. But what they don't know is that if I wanted to I
    could be like the water of a torrent that would sweep
    them away.

*One of the sisters enters and goes out carrying a loaf of
bread.*

MARIA: Even so, I'm sure your husband still loves you.
YERMA: He gives me bread and a roof.
MARIA: What misery you're going through! What misery!
    But think of the wounds of Our Lord.

Yerma and Maria are at the doorway.

YERMA *(Looking at the baby)*: He's wakened up.
MARIA: He'll start singing in a minute.
YERMA: Your eyes. Had you noticed that? Did you see?
    (Crying) He has your eyes, your eyes!

*Yerma gently pushes Maria, who goes out silently. Yerma
turns toward the door through which her husband went
out.*

GIRL 2: Ssss!

YERMA *(Turning)*: What?

GIRL 2: I was waiting for you to come out. My mother's waiting for you.

YERMA: Is she alone?

GIRL 2: With two women, neighbors.

YERMA: Ask her to wait for a minute.

GIRL 2: But you'll go? You're not afraid?

YERMA: I'll go.

GIRL 2: It's up to you!

YERMA: Tell them to wait, even if it gets late!

Victor enters.

VICTOR: Is Juan here?

YERMA: Yes.

GIRL 2 *(Conspiratorial)*: Well, I'll bring the dress, then.

YERMA: Whenever you like.

The girl goes.

Sit down.

VICTOR: I'm all right.

YERMA *(Calling)*: Juan!

VICTOR: I've come to say goodbye. *(He shivers slightly, but regains his calm)*

YERMA: Are you going with your brothers?

VICTOR: That's what my father wants.

YERMA: He must be an old man.

VICTOR: He is. Very old.

Pause.

YERMA: It's a good thing to change pastures.

VICTOR: They're all the same.

YERMA: No. I'd go a long way from here.

VICTOR: It's the same everywhere. The same sheep give the same wool.

YERMA: That's how it is for men. With women it's different. I've never heard a man say, while he was eating, "What good apples these are." You go straight for what you want without stopping for pleasantries. But when it comes to me, I can tell you I loathe the water of the wells around here.

VICTOR: That's possible.

The scene is in a soft half-light.

YERMA: Victor.

VICTOR: What is it?

YERMA: Why are you going? People like you here.

VICTOR: I did my best.

Pause.

YERMA: You did your best. When you were hardly grown-up you carried me in your arms once, do you remember? You never know how things are going to turn out.

VICTOR: Everything changes.

YERMA: Some things don't. There are things locked up behind walls that never change because nobody hears them.

VICTOR: That's how it is.

The second sister appears and moves slowly toward the door, where she stands still, lit by the last evening light.

YERMA: But if they were to come out all at once and shout, they'd fill the whole world.

VICTOR: It wouldn't do any good. The ditch in its banks, the flock in the fold, the moon in heaven and the man at his plow.

YERMA: How we suffer for not heeding the sayings of the old!

The long melancholy notes of the shepherds' conches can be heard.

VICTOR: The flocks.

JUAN *(Coming in)*: Are you on your way?

VICTOR: I want to get through the mountains before morning.

JUAN: Have you any complaints against me?

VICTOR: No. You paid me what you owed me.

JUAN *(To Yerma)*: I bought his sheep.

YERMA: Did you?

VICTOR *(To Yerma)*: They're yours.

YERMA: I didn't know.

JUAN *(Satisfied)*: That's how it is.

VICTOR: Your husband's farm will be overflowing.

YERMA: The fruit falls to the hands that work for it.

The sister who is standing in the doorway goes out.

JUAN: There's already not enough room for all those sheep.

YERMA *(Darkly)*: The earth is wide.

Pause.

JUAN: We can walk as far as the stream together.

VICTOR: I wish great happiness on this house. *(He holds out his hand to Yerma)*
YERMA: May God hear you! And keep you!

Victor starts out. At an imperceptible movement of Yerma's, he turns.

VICTOR: Did you say something?
YERMA *(Dramatically)*: I said, "God keep you."
VICTOR: Thank you.

They go. Yerma stands looking in anguish at the hand which Victor had held. Yerma turns quickly to the left and takes up a shawl.

GIRL 2: Come. *(Covering her head silently)*
YERMA: Come.

They go out, without a sound.
The stage is almost dark. The first sister enters with an oil lamp (which should bring no more light than its own onto the set). She goes to the other end of the stage looking for Yerma. The conches of the shepherds can be heard.

FIRST SISTER-IN-LAW *(In a hushed voice)*: Yerma!

The second sister enters. They look at each other and turn toward the door.

SECOND SISTER-IN-LAW *(Louder)*: Yerma!
FIRST SISTER-IN-LAW *(Stepping toward the door; in an imperious voice)*: Yerma!

The sounds of the shepherds' conches and horns are heard.
The stage is very dark.
   Curtain.

Act Three

SCENE ONE

House of Dolores the witch. Daybreak. Yerma enters with Dolores and two old women.

DOLORES: I see you don't frighten easily.

OLD WOMAN 1: There's no force in the world that's as strong as desire.

OLD WOMAN 2: But it was too dark in the cemetery.

DOLORES: Many many times I've pronounced those prayers in the cemetery with women who wanted children and they were always afraid. Except you.

YERMA: I came for the result. I don't believe you'd cheat me.

DOLORES: I wouldn't. May my tongue fill with ants like the mouths of the dead if I have ever once lied. The last time I pronounced those prayers with a beggar woman who's been barren longer than you and her womb was freshened so beautifully that she was brought to birth of two babies down there at the river, because she didn't have time to get home, and she brought them back up here herself, wrapped up in a cloth, for me to see to them.

YERMA: She was able to walk up here from the river?

DOLORES: She managed. Her shoes and her petticoat were full of blood . . . but her face was shining.

YERMA: Nothing happened to her?

DOLORES: What could happen to her? God is God.

YERMA: Of course. God is God. Nothing could have happened to her. Just pick up the babies and wash them in the running water. The animals lick them, don't they? I wouldn't be disgusted if it was my own baby. I think a woman who's just given birth must be as though there were lights inside her, and the babies sleep on her for hours and hours hearing the stream of warm milk flowing into the breasts for them to suck and to play with until they don't want any more and turn their heads away. "Another little bit, baby, a little more . . . " and the breast, and his face, are covered with the white drops.

DOLORES: Now you'll have a baby. I promise you.

YERMA: I'll have one because I must have one. Or else I don't understand the world. Sometimes, when I'm convinced that never, never . . . it's as though a wave of fire flowed up through me starting in my feet, and afterwards everything looked empty to me, and the men in the street and the bulls and the stones looked to me as though they were made out of cotton. And then I'd ask myself, what were they all put there for?

OLD WOMAN 1: A wife ought to want children, but if she doesn't have them, why this terrible passion for them? The important thing in this world is to let the years carry you along. I'm not blaming you. You saw: I joined in on the prayers. But what green fields do you think you can give a child, or what happiness, or what silver chair?

YERMA: I don't think about tomorrow, I think about today. You're old. To you everything is like a book you've read. I think about how I'm thirsty, and how I'm not free. I want to hold my child in my arms so that I can sleep in peace. And listen to me, and don't be shocked at what I say: Even if I knew that my child would be cruel to me later and would hate me and drag me through the streets by my hair, I'd be happy when he was born, because it's much much better to cry because a living man runs knives into you than to cry because of his ghost that's been sitting year after year on my heart.

OLD WOMAN 1: You're too young to listen to advice. But while you're waiting for the grace of God you should take refuge in your husband's love.

YERMA: Oh! There you've touched the deepest pain of my body.

DOLORES: Your husband's a good man.

YERMA *(Standing up)*: Good! He's good! What difference does that make? I wish he were bad. But no. He takes his flock along the sheep tracks and at night he counts his money. When he sleeps with me he does his duty but I can feel how cold he is around the middle, as though he were a dead man. I was always disgusted by hot women, but at that moment I wish I were a mountain of fire.

DOLORES: Yerma!

YERMA: I'm not an indecent wife. But I know that children are born of a man and a woman. Oh, if only I could have them by myself!

DOLORES: Remember that your husband suffers too.

YERMA: No he doesn't. He doesn't want children.

OLD WOMAN 1: Don't say such a thing!

YERMA: I can see it in his eyes. And since he doesn't want
them he doesn't give me any. I don't love him, I don't
love him, and yet he's my only salvation. For my
honor, and the name I was born with. My only
salvation.

OLD WOMAN 1 *(Frightened)*: It'll be day soon. You must go
home.

DOLORES: The flocks will soon be going out. It wouldn't be
good if you were seen alone.

YERMA: I had to talk about it. To let it come out. How
many times should I repeat the prayers?

DOLORES: The prayer of the laurel twice, and at noon the
prayer of Saint Ann. When you know you're pregnant
bring me the bushel-and-a-half of wheat that you
promised me.

OLD WOMAN 1: There's the first light on the top of the
mountains. Go.

DOLORES: They'll be opening the gates of the courtyards.
Go around the back way, by the stream.

YERMA *(Discouraged)*: I don't know what I came for!

DOLORES: Are you sorry you came?

YERMA: No!

DOLORES *(Troubled)*: If you're afraid, I'll go with you as far
as the bend.

FIRST WOMAN *(Worried)*: It'll be broad daylight by the time
you get to your doorway.

The sound of voices.

DOLORES: Hush!

They listen.

FIRST WOMAN: Nobody there. God be with you.

Yerma starts toward the door, and at the same moment, someone calls her name. The three women stand still.

DOLORES: Who is it?
JUAN *(Off)*: It's I.
YERMA: Open the door.

Dolores hesitates.

Are you going to open it?

Murmurs from outside. Juan and the two sisters-in-law appear.

SECOND SISTER: Here she is.
YERMA: Here I am.
JUAN: What are you doing in this place? If I could shout I'd rouse the whole village to come and see what had become of the honor of my house, but I have to throttle it and keep quiet because you're my wife.
YERMA: And if I could shout I would, to rouse the dead themselves to come and see the innocence that surrounds me.
JUAN: No! Not that! I've put up with everything, but that I won't. You're unfaithful to me, you make a fool of me, and I'm just a man who works the land, I can't keep up with your ins and outs!
DOLORES: Juan!

JUAN: Not a word out of you!

DOLORES *(Loudly)*: Your wife hasn't done anything wrong!

JUAN: She has! Since the very day we were married.
Looking at me with two needles, lying awake at night
with her eyes open beside me, and covering my
pillows with her dreadful sighs.

YERMA: Be quiet!

JUAN: And I can't stand any more. You'd have to be made
of brass to be able to live with a woman who kept
trying to get her fingers into your heart and who went
out of the house at night looking—for what? Tell me!
What is it you go looking for? The streets are full of
males. There aren't any flowers to pick there.

YERMA: I won't hear another word. Not one other word.
You think that you and your people are the only ones
who care about protecting your honor, and you like to
forget that no one of my name ever had anything to
hide. Come here. Smell my clothes. Come here!
Come and see if there's any smell on them but yours,
the smell of your body. Take me out in the square
and strip me naked and spit at me. Do what you like
with me. I'm your wife. But don't try to hang the
name of a man on my breasts.

JUAN: It is not I who do that, it's you, the way you behave.
It's the village that says it. They're starting to say it
clearly. When I go up to a few of them they all stop
talking. When I go to weigh the flour they all stop
talking. Even at night, in the fields, when I wake up I
think the branches of the trees have just stopped
talking.

YERMA: I don't know where the bad winds come from that
flatten the wheat, but the wheat can be good just the
same.

JUAN: And I don't know what a woman can be looking for
    away from her house at all hours.

YERMA *(In a sudden passion, embracing her husband)*: I'm
    looking for you! It's you I'm looking for. It's you I
    look for day and night without finding a shadow
    where I could breathe. It's your blood and your help
    that I want.

JUAN: Get away.

YERMA: Don't push me off. Love me!

JUAN: Let go of me!

YERMA: Look how alone I am. As though the moon went
    through the sky looking for herself. Look at me! *(She
    looks at him)*

JUAN *(Looks at her and roughly shoves her away from him)*:
    Once and for all, let me alone!

DOLORES: Juan!

Yerma falls to the floor.

YERMA *(Loudly)*: When I went out to pick my carnations I
    ran into a wall. Oh! Oh! This is the wall I have to
    dash my head against.

JUAN: Be still. Come, we're going.

DOLORES: My God!

YERMA *(Shouting)*: A curse on my father who gave me his
    father's blood that had come down through a hundred
    sons. A curse on my blood that goes beating on the
    walls looking for them.

JUAN: I said be still!

DOLORES: There are people coming. Keep your voice
    down.

YERMA: I don't care. Let my voice be free at least, now that
    I'm going to the bottom of the well. *(She gets up)* Let

this one beautiful thing at least come out of my body
and fill the air.

Voices are heard.

DOLORES: They're coming past here.

JUAN: Be quiet.

YERMA: That's it! That's it! Quiet. Never fear.

JUAN: Come. Right now!

YERMA: That's that! That's that! No use wringing my
hands! It's one thing to want something with your
head . . .

JUAN: Be quiet.

YERMA *(Lowering her voice)*: It's one thing to want something
with your head and it's another thing when the
body—I curse the body—won't respond. It's written,
and I'm not going to wrestle with the tide. That's
that! Not a word out of me now, not a word! *(She
goes)*

Rapid Curtain.

SCENE TWO

*The surroundings of a hermitage, high in the mountains. In the
farmyard several cartwheels and blankets form a rustic tent.
Yerma is inside it. Barefoot women enter with offerings for the
hermitage. The happy old woman of the first act is also onstage.*

SONG
   (Before the curtain rises)
   When you were single

I couldn't see you,
Now that you're married
I'll meet you.
Wife and pilgrim
I'll take off your clothes
In the dark
As it strikes twelve.

FIRST OLD WOMAN *(Lazily)*: Have you drunk the holy water?

WOMAN 1: Yes.

FIRST OLD WOMAN: Now let's see what he can do.

WOMAN 1: We believe in him.

FIRST OLD WOMAN: You come to the Saint to ask for babies and as a result every year more single men come on this pilgrimage. What do you make of that? *(She laughs)*

WOMAN 1: What did you come for if you don't believe?

FIRST OLD WOMAN: To watch. I'm mad to watch. And to keep an eye on my son. Last year there were two of them killed each other over a barren wife and I want to keep a lookout. And after all I come because I like to.

WOMAN 1: God forgive you!

They go in.

FIRST OLD WOMAN *(Sarcastically)*: May He forgive you.

The old woman goes. Maria enters with the first girl.

GIRL 1: Has she come?

MARIA: There's the cart. I had a hard time getting them

here. She hadn't got out of her chair for a month.
She frightens me. She's got some idea I can't make
out, but I know it's a bad one.

GIRL 1: I came with my sister. She's been coming for eight
years without it doing any good.

MARIA: The ones that want babies get them.

GIRL 1: That's what I say.

The sound of voices.

MARIA: I never liked this pilgrimage. Let's go down to the
threshing floor. That's where they all are.

GIRL 1: Last year when it got dark some boys grabbed my
sister's breasts and almost tore them off.

MARIA: For miles around you hear nothing but horrors.

GIRL 1: I've seen over forty barrels of wine in back of the
hermitage.

MARIA: There's a river of single men coming down from
the mountains.

*The girl goes. The sound of voices. Yerma enters with six
women on their way to church. They are barefoot and
carrying fluted candles. Night begins to fall.*

Lord, may the rose flower.
Leave not my rose in the shadow.

WOMAN 2:
On her barren flesh
May the yellow rose flower.

MARIA:
And in the womb of thy servants
The dark flame of the earth.

CHORUS OF WOMEN:
> Lord, may the rose flower.
> Leave not my rose in the shadow.

They kneel.

YERMA:
> There are gardens in heaven
> With rose trees of joy,
> And among the roses
> The rose of wonder,
> Like a ray of dawn;
> An archangel guards it,
> His wings like torments,
> His eyes like agonies.
> Around the petals
> Streams of warm milk
> Play and wet the faces
> Of the tranquil stars.
> Lord, open thy rose tree
> Over my barren flesh.

They rise.

WOMAN 2:
> Lord, soothe with thy hand
> The embers of her cheek.

YERMA:
> Hear the penitent
> Of thy holy pilgrimage.
> Open thy rose in my flesh
> Though it have a thousand thorns.

CHORUS OF WOMEN:
> Lord, may the rose flower.
> Leave not my rose in the shadow.

YERMA:
> Over my barren flesh
> The rose of wonder.

They all go in.

> *Girls come running in from the left with long ribbons in their hands. From the right, three other girls enter, looking backward. Onstage a crescendo of voices and the noise of cattle bells and harness bells. On an upper level seven girls appear waving their ribbons to the left. The noise increases, and two figures of popular tradition enter—a male and a female. They are wearing large masks. The male figure is holding a bull's horn. They are in no way grotesque, but of great beauty, and redolent of the earth itself. The female shakes a collar of harness bells. The upper part of the stage fills with people who shout and comment on the dance. It has grown very dark.*

CHILDREN: The devil and his wife! The devil and his wife!

FEMALE:
> In the mountain river
> The sad wife was bathing.
> The water snails
> Climbed up her body.
> The sand of the banks
> And the morning breeze
> Kindled her laugh

So her shoulders shook.
Ay, how naked she was,
The girl in the water!

CHILD:

Oh, how unhappy she was!

MAN 1:

Oh, emptied of love
By the wind and the water!

MAN 2:

Let her say what she hopes for!

MAN 1:

Let her say what she's waiting for!

MAN 2:

Oh, with the dry womb
And the skin of no color!

FEMALE:

When night comes I will tell her,
When the clear night comes.
When night comes to the pilgrimage
I'll tear the pleats of my skirt.

CHILD:

And right then the night came.
Oh, but the night came!
Look at the mountain stream,
How it's turned black!

Guitars begin.

MALE *(Rising and shaking the horn)*:
Oh how white
The sad bride!
Oh how she mourns among the branches!
Later she'll be poppy and carnation
When the male unfurls his cloak.

(He approaches)

If you come of the pilgrimage
Asking that your womb may open,
Do not come wearing mourning
But a dress of fine Holland linen.
Go alone behind the walls
Of the gardens of fig trees
And hold up my body of earth
Till the white groan of dawn.
Oh, how she shines!
Oh, how she was shining!
Oh, how the bride flashes!

FEMALE:
Oh, may love set on her head
Wreaths and garlands,
And in her breast
Fix darts of bright gold.

MALE:
Seven times she groaned,
Nine times she rose up,
Fifteen times the jasmine
Mingled with the oranges.

MAN 3:
> Now give her the horn!

MAN 2:
> With the rose and the dance!

MAN 1:
> Oh, how the bride flashes!

MALE:
> On this pilgrimage
> It's always the man who commands.
> The husbands are bulls.
> It's always the man who commands
> And the pilgrims are flowers
> For him that plucks them.

CHILD:
> Now give her the wind!

MAN 2:
> Now give her the branch!

MALE:
> Come, see how the light shines
> Out of the one that was bathing!

MAN 1:
> She bends like a reed.

FEMALE:
> She languishes like a flower.

ALL MEN:
> Send the little girls away.

MALE:

> Let the dance blaze up
> And the shining body
> Of the spotless bride.

Everyone exits, dancing to the sound of hand-clapping and laughter. They sing:

ALL:

> There are gardens in heaven
> With rose trees of joy,
> And among the roses
> The rose of wonder.

Two girls come back through shouting. The happy old woman enters.

FIRST OLD WOMAN: Maybe you'll let us sleep in a little while. But then it'll be her.

Yerma enters.

You!

Yerma is extremely dejected and says nothing.

Tell me, what did you come for?

YERMA: I don't know.

FIRST OLD WOMAN: Aren't you convinced yet? And your husband?

Yerma makes a gesture of fatigue, of someone who is obsessed with a single idea.

YERMA: He's there.

FIRST OLD WOMAN: What's he doing?

YERMA: Drinking. *(Pause. She raises her hands to her forehead)* Ay!

FIRST OLD WOMAN: Ay! Ay! Less "ay!" and more soul. I couldn't tell you anything before, but now I can.

YERMA: What can you tell me that I don't know?

FIRST OLD WOMAN: What can't be kept quiet. What shouts from the rooftops. It's your husband's fault. Do you hear? They can cut off my hands if it isn't. Neither his father nor his grandfather nor his great-grandfather behaved like men of breeding. For them to have a baby the heavens had to come down to the earth, because they're made out of nothing but spit. But your people aren't like that. You've got brothers and cousins for a hundred miles around. Look at the curse that's fallen on your beauty.

YERMA: A curse. A flood of poison on the tasseled corn.

FIRST OLD WOMAN: But you have feet. You can leave your house.

YERMA: Leave it?

FIRST OLD WOMAN: When I saw you on the pilgrimage it made my heart turn over. This is where women come to meet new men. And the Saint works a miracle. My son's waiting for you behind the hermitage. My house needs a woman. Go with him. We'll live together, the three of us. My son comes of good blood, like me. If you come into my house you can still smell the cradles. The ash of your bedclothes will turn into bread and salt for your babies. Go. Never mind about anyone else. As for your husband, there's enough guts and iron in my house so that he won't even dare cross the street.

YERMA: Be still! Be still, what are you saying! I'd never do that. I can't go looking for anything. Do you imagine that I could know another man? And what an idea you have of my honor! The water can't flow backwards nor the full moon come out at noon. Go. I've started on my own way and I'll go on with it. Did you seriously think I could give myself to another man? Did you think I could go and ask him for what's mine, as though I were a slave? Get to know me, so you'll know better than to talk to me anymore. I don't go looking for anything.

FIRST OLD WOMAN: When you're thirsty, water tastes good.

YERMA: I'm like a dry field that would need a thousand pairs of oxen to plow it, and you offer me a little glass of well water. My suffering isn't even in my body anymore.

FIRST OLD WOMAN *(Loudly)*: Well, go on like that, then. That's what you want. Like the thistles on the sand hills, all prickly and barren.

YERMA *(Loudly)*: Barren, yes! I know it! Barren! You don't have to fling it in my face. Don't stand over me enjoying it like children watching the death of some little animal. Ever since I was married I've been going around and around that word, but this is the first time that anyone's said it to my face. The first time that I see it's true.

FIRST OLD WOMAN: I've no pity for you. None at all. I'll go find another woman for my son.

The old woman goes. In the distance a large chorus of pilgrims is heard singing. Yerma turns toward the cart and her husband appears from behind it.

YERMA: Were you there all along?

JUAN: I was.

YERMA: Spying on me?

JUAN: Spying on you.

YERMA: And did you hear?

JUAN: Yes.

YERMA: Well? Let me alone. Go down to the singing. *(She sits on the blankets)*

JUAN: Now it's my turn to speak.

YERMA: Speak!

JUAN: And make my own complaint.

YERMA: What about?

JUAN: My throat's full of bitterness.

YERMA: So are my bones.

JUAN: I've endured all that I can of this continuous lament for dark things that are outside of life, for things that are in the air.

YERMA *(With theatrical astonishment)*: Outside of life, you say? In the air, you say?

JUAN: For things that haven't happened, that neither you nor I can control.

YERMA *(Violently)*: Go on, go on!

JUAN: For things that aren't important to me. Do you hear? They aren't important to me. I must tell you that now. What matters to me is what I have in my hands. What I can see with my eyes.

YERMA *(Getting up onto her knees, desperate)*: That's it, that's it. That's what I wanted to hear from your lips. . . . The truth's hard to hear when it's inside somebody, but how loud it shouts when it comes out and lifts up its arms. It doesn't matter to him! Now I've heard him!

JUAN *(Approaching her)*: Tell yourself it had to be the way it is. Listen to me. *(He embraces her, trying to draw her to*

her feet) Many women would be happy to live the way
you do. Life's sweeter without children. I'm happy not
to have any. It's not our fault.

YERMA: And what did you want from me?

JUAN: Yourself.

YERMA *(Excitedly)*: That's it! You wanted a house, peace
and quiet, and a wife. But nothing more. Is that true,
what I've said?

JUAN: It's true. Like everybody else.

YERMA: And the rest? And your son?

JUAN *(Loudly)*: Didn't you hear me. That doesn't matter to
me. Don't go on asking me about it! Must I shout it
in your ear to get you to understand it! Maybe now
you'll live in peace, finally.

YERMA: And you never thought of a son when you saw how
much I wanted one?

JUAN: Never.

They are both on the ground.

YERMA: And I can't hope for one?

JUAN: No.

YERMA: And you can't either?

JUAN: No I can't. Resign yourself.

YERMA: Barren!

JUAN: And we'll live in peace. The two of us, pleasantly,
happily. Put your arms around me.

She does.

YERMA: What do you want?

JUAN: You. You're beautiful in the moonlight.

YERMA: You want me the way sometimes you want to eat a
pigeon.

JUAN: Kiss me . . . that way.
YERMA: That never. Never.

> *Yerma shrieks and clutches her husband by the throat. He falls backward. She grips his throat until he dies. The chorus of pilgrims begins singing.*

Barren, barren, but sure. Now I know it for certain. And I'm alone.

> *She rises. People begin to enter.*

I'm going to sleep without suddenly waking up wondering whether I felt a new blood in my blood. My body's barren forever. What do you want? Don't come near, because I've killed my son, I've killed my son with my own hands!

> *A group gathers, but remains upstage. The chorus of pilgrims can be heard.*
> Curtain.

1920
El Maleficio de la Mariposa

1923
Mariana Pineda

1926
La zapatera prodigiosa

1928
Los Títeres de cachiporra
Amor de Don Perlimplín con Belisa en su jardín

1929–30
Así que pasen cinco años

1930
El público

1931
Retabillo de Don Cristóbal

1933
Bodas de Sangre

1934
Yerma

1935
Doña Rosita la soltera, o El lenguaje de las flores

1936
La casa de Bernarda Alba

THE TRANSLATORS

LANGSTON HUGHES, born in Joplin, Missouri in 1902, wrote more than sixty volumes of prose, poetry, plays, librettos, songs and children's stories, and translated the poetry of various Latin American and Spanish writers, most notably Nicolás Guillén and Federico García Lorca. Among his many honors was his election to the National Institute of Arts and Letters in 1961. He died in 1967.

W. S. MERWIN, born in New York City in 1927, is a poet, playwright, and translator of Spanish, French, Latin and Portuguese literature. His numerous volumes of poetry include *The Carrier of Ladders* (1970), for which he was awarded the Pulitzer Prize. Winner of the P.E.N. Translation Prize in 1968 for his *Selected Translations 1948–1968*, he was awarded the Fellowship of the Academy of American Poets in 1974. In 1987, he received the Governor's Award for Literature of the State of Hawaii, where he currently resides.

MELIA BENSUSSEN, a native Spanish speaker, is a director and translator. For many years an Artist-in-Residence at the New York Shakespeare Festival, where she directed the premiere production of the Langston Hughes translation of *Blood Wedding*, she has directed extensively in New York City and in resident theatres throughout the United States.